AWAKEN YOUR HIGHER SELF

10 Laws to Unlock Your Inner Power
and Discover Your True Calling

You were guided here for a reason. It's the calling of your Higher Self

VIKASH RASHINKAR

Awaken Your Higer Self

Copyright © 2025 Vikash Rashinkar

All rights reserved. No part of this book may be reproduced, stored in a retrieval system, or transmitted in any form or by any means, electronic, mechanical, photocopying, recording, or otherwise, without the prior written permission of the author.

This book is sold as is, without any warranties, express or implied. The author and publisher are not responsible for any problems that may arise from using this book. If you have a problem with the book, your only option is to return it for a refund. The author agrees to protect the publisher from any legal issues that may arise from the book's content. Any legal disputes about this book will be handled according to the laws of the constitution of India

Publisher: Inkscribe Publishing Pvt. Ltd

ISBN Number: 978-1-969259-23-4

Contents

"The Inner Whisper That Brought You Here"

Acknowledgments 5
How This Book Can Work Miracles In Your Life 7

1. Understanding The Higher Self & Ego The Journey Begins Within 13
2. Signs Of Spiritual Awakening 26
3. Mindfulness & Present-Moment Awareness 47
4. Remembering Who You Are 77
5. Nature Connection & Silence 100
6. Gratitude & Positive Affirmations 106
7. Healing The Past & Releasing Pain 146
8. Aligning Energy, Aura, And Values 199
9. Intuition, Synchronicity & Inner Guidance 232
10. Service, Giving Back & Community 261

Key Takeaways That Helped Me In Difficult Times 281
10 Laws To Unlock Your Inner God And Find Your True Calling 283
Shukrana 285

Acknowledgments

With deepest gratitude, I thank my **parents,** whose love, strength, and silent sacrifices are the roots of everything I am becoming. Your unwavering support, patience, and belief in me, even in the moments I could not believe in myself, have carried me through more than you know.

To my **elders** and my beloved **grandmother,** thank you for your blessings, wisdom, and prayers that have shielded me in countless invisible ways. Your presence has been a sacred pillar in my life. I also wish to thank my **elder cousin sister and brother,** whose emotional presence and quiet encouragement were often the light I needed during the dimmest hours of my path.

A special and sacred thank you to my **auntie, G. Manonmani,** and **uncle, S. Govardangiri.** When I was at my lowest, mentally, physically, and spiritually, you stood by me. You became the healing force in my life. You didn't just help me survive, you helped me remember why life was worth living. This book is born of that healing. It is a living testimony to your love, compassion, and divine timing.

To the **Higher Divine,** the ever-present source behind all life, and to my **Higher Self,** the part of me that never gave up even when I did, thank you for guiding me home through intuition, silence, and truth.

And to **Guruji,** whose teachings and presence have become the compass of my inner world, thank you for reminding me of who I truly am.

With all my heart,
Vikash Rashinkar

How This Book Can Work Miracles In Your Life

This is not just a book, it's a force. A living, breathing field of transformation that holds the power to shift your reality, awaken your sleeping potential, and align you with the divine frequency of who you truly are. Whether you feel lost or lit up, broken or blooming, these words carry energy. The moment you begin reading, something starts to stir. A quiet inner voice grows louder. Your breath slows. Your soul listens.

This book is timeless. It's not confined to the version of you reading it today, it's also written for the version of you five years from now, ten years from now, and even the one who hasn't yet dared to dream. Whenever you return to these pages, they'll offer exactly what your soul needs. It's as if the book knows you. Because it does. It was **manifested and blessed** to meet you, transform you, and remind you: *You were never ordinary.* You are powerful. You are chosen. And this, right here, is the spark that will awaken your inner god.

How to Use This Book

Don't just read this book, **feel** it. Let the words enter not only your mind, but your heart and spirit. Read slowly. Let each sentence breathe inside you. This isn't something to rush through. This is your **sacred manual**, your mirror, your mentor.

Each time you open this book, you'll find new meaning, because every chapter speaks to a deeper version of you. Use it like a compass. A ritual. A soul tune-up. Practice the laws. Reflect on the insights. Allow the vibration of the words to expand your aura and lift your state of being. You'll begin to notice signs, patterns, synchronicities. This is not a coincidence. That's your Higher Self responding.

Journal your thoughts. Embrace the practices. Observe the quiet miracles that begin to unfold around you. This book is your key to unlocking a life filled with power, peace, purpose, and the unshakable presence of your truest, most radiant self.

Unique Features of This Book

This book is unlike anything you've encountered before. It doesn't just teach, it **activates**. Every chapter is embedded with an energetic signature that wakes up something ancient and powerful inside of you. These aren't just lessons, they're codes. Codes that help you decode your own soul, amplify your energy, and step into the life you were born to live.

You'll discover how to command your thoughts, direct your energy, and master your emotional frequency. It's a fusion of spiritual truth, psychological insight, and intuitive wisdom, crafted to help you rise. Not once. Not temporarily. But permanently.

The teachings within are designed to **rewire your reality**, from survival to sovereignty. These tools won't just inspire you for a moment, they'll empower you for a lifetime. This is your guide to mastering your inner world, magnetizing your desires, and awakening the divine intelligence that lives within you.

The Reason Behind This Book

The world is overflowing with information, yet people feel more lost than ever. Anxious minds. Unfulfilled hearts. Souls disconnected from their truth. We scroll endlessly. We chase what doesn't satisfy us. And at the root of it all is a forgotten truth: *we've lost touch with our inner power.*

This book was created to restore that connection. It is the result of years of soul-searching, deep research, and life-tested wisdom. It's not just a book, it's a **response** to the quiet pain of the world and the untapped greatness inside you.

Throughout history, in every age, there were sacred texts and epics written to guide people back to their essence. Stories and systems that lit the way when everything seemed dark. This book stands on that legacy, modernized for this era, simplified for this generation, yet just as eternal in its truth.

It is here to wake you up. To shake you from slumber. To remind you of who you are and why you came. If you're holding this book, it's not by chance. You are ready.

The Flow State: Where Time Stops and Your Greatness Begins

There exists a sacred moment where time disappears and your entire being becomes one with the task at hand. Your actions become effortless. Your thoughts are crystal clear. Doubts dissolve. You feel *alive*. This is the flow state, a portal to your highest potential.

When you enter the flow, you don't try to succeed, you become successful. Whether you're painting, building, moving, creating, or simply being, the flow state is your soul whispering: *this is it*.

Flow is not an accident, it's a frequency. And you can learn to access it on command. With intention, presence, and the tools you'll discover in this book, you'll learn how to drop into flow, unlock your brilliance, and live from a state of **natural magic**.

This book will show you how to tune your energy to the rhythm of life, where happiness isn't something you chase, but something you tap into. Once you experience that harmony, that alignment, nothing else compares.

GOD MODE: The Ultimate State of Power, Focus, and Flow

There is a rare, sacred state where everything clicks. Time stretches. Your body, mind, and soul are unified. There is no overthinking, no hesitation, just forward motion. **That state is God Mode.**

Much like the hidden settings in a computer that unlock full control, God Mode in life is the state where you access **total clarity, limitless energy, and divine presence.** You feel *invincible*, not in ego, but in soul. It's not about superiority. It's about alignment. It's about operating from your full potential, fully alive, fully aware, fully unstoppable.

God Mode is that fire in your belly, the peace in your heart, and the electricity in your soul, all working in perfect rhythm. And yes, you've touched it before, in those fleeting moments of deep focus, pure love, wild creativity, or fearless action.

This book will teach you how to enter that state, not by accident, but by design. You'll discover how to build the habits, rituals, and mindset that make this state your **default**. You won't need to chase greatness. You'll *embody* it.

Wonders Happen When You Start Reading This Book to Your Heart

Something miraculous happens when you stop reading with your eyes and start reading with your heart. That's when the book begins to speak *through you*. That's when transformation begins.

You'll start to notice the shift. Your thoughts become lighter. Your body feels more alive. Your energy becomes magnetic. The world starts responding to you in mysterious, beautiful ways. Because you're no longer waiting for miracles, you've become one.

This book will show you how to return to the most powerful place of all: *within*. It will teach you how to awaken your Higher Self, expand your aura, unlock divine wisdom, and connect with the **inner god** that's always been waiting.

From this space, you no longer seek. You create. You no longer chase. You attract. You no longer doubt. You *know*.

This is not the end of a chapter. It's the beginning of your new life.

A life led by the soul. A life lived in truth. A life powered by your divine essence.

Welcome home.

THE AWAKENING BEGINS

1

Understanding The Higher Self & Ego The Journey Begins Within

When the Soul Begins to Whisper

Every great transformation doesn't begin with a loud bang, it begins with a whisper. A quiet ache in your chest. A question that won't leave your mind.

"Who am I, really?"

"Why does something feel… missing?"

"Why do I sense there's more to life than this?" or even "What is the purpose of living?"

These questions aren't breakdowns, they're breakthroughs waiting to happen. They are echoes from a deeper part of you, your **Higher Self**, stirring beneath the surface. That voice within has waited patiently, letting you live, stumble, succeed, and even forget. But now, it calls louder, not with noise, but with *knowing*.

And if you're reading these words right now, it means you heard that call. You are not here by accident. The book found you because your spirit is ready to remember. Ready to rise.

The Real You Beneath It All

The Higher Self is not a myth. It's not reserved for saints, gurus, or mystics. It is the **eternal intelligence within you** the You that existed before fear entered, before the world handed you roles, rules, and reasons to hide.

You've already met this version of yourself. In moments of stillness. In moments of deep truth. When you felt completely aligned, peaceful, and powerful without needing anyone's approval. That was your Higher Self in command.

The Higher Self is your access to the **divine subconscious mind**, the limitless field where your beliefs shape your reality, and your inner dialogue becomes your destiny. It is the inner source that says:

"You are not broken. You are becoming."

The Mask Called Ego

But just as the Higher Self whispers truth, another voice often shouts over it. That voice is the **Ego**.

It pretends to protect you, but in truth, it imprisons you. It creates stories built on fear, comparison, pride, and shame. It says, *"You must control everything. You must win. You must be seen, or you are nothing."*

Sometimes, the Ego even disguises itself as "spiritual growth", inflating you with pride for simply reading books, meditating, or appearing awakened. But the moment you feel superior, you've already stepped out of truth and into illusion.

The Ego feeds on fear. The Higher Self feeds on love.

The Ego reacts. The Higher Self responds.

The Ego demands applause. The Higher Self walks in silence, knowing it is already whole.

But let's not villainize the Ego, it's a scarred protector. It formed when you were young, trying to shield you from pain. It helped you survive. But now? It's time to *thrive*.

When the Subconscious Becomes Your Superpower

Deep inside your mind, beneath conscious thought, lies your **subconscious mind**, the seat of beliefs, habits, and automatic responses. What you believe on this level becomes law in your life. That is why your inner dialogue matters.

The subconscious does not argue. It accepts. If you constantly say, *"I'm not enough,"* it will orchestrate your reality to prove you right. But when your Higher Self becomes your internal commander, your thoughts shift. And the subconscious, like fertile soil, begins to grow new, empowering truths.

This book is your tool to rewrite the code. To install a new operating system. One where your inner world creates miracles effortlessly, because your **Higher Self** and **subconscious mind** are in harmony.

The Illusion of Power vs. True Power

In a world obsessed with domination, control, and performance, we are often told that power means *outsmarting, outshining, outperforming*. But true power isn't loud. It's **presence**.

Your Higher Self doesn't manipulate,it magnetizes. It doesn't grasp,it receives. It doesn't compare,it creates.

When you move from Ego-based control to Higher-Self alignment, you stop chasing power and begin radiating it. You become a living law of nature,still, yet unstoppable. This is real charisma. This is unshakeable influence. It doesn't demand the room's attention. It *commands* it,silently, fully.

The Shift: A Sacred Turning Point

Understanding these two inner voices,Ego and Higher Self,is your first awakening. But knowing is not enough. The shift begins when you **choose** differently, moment by moment.

Each time you respond with compassion instead of control, you strengthen your divine identity.

Each time you move with intention instead of impulse, you train your energy to align with your truth.

This is not easy. But it is holy.

It's the journey from fear to freedom. From survival to soulfulness.

The Story: The Mirror in the Mountain

In the quiet shadow of the Western Ghats, there lived a boy named Prakash. Though bright and kind, he lived under a storm of self-doubt. He constantly looked outside for approval, listening to the loud, mocking voice of Ego:

"You're not enough unless they praise you."

One day, an old monk approached and said, *"There's a sacred mirror hidden in the mountain. It reflects who you truly are. Go find it."*

With nothing but hope and hunger, Prakash climbed. The journey was harsh. Every fall stripped away a false identity his need to impress, his fear of judgment, his belief that worth is earned.

At last, he found the cave. But there was no mirror. Just silence. He sat down. Closed his eyes. And then, he heard it. A voice from within, soft and wise:

"The mirror is not outside you. It is your awareness. Still your mind, and you will see."

Tears streamed down his face. For the first time, he saw himself, not through others, but through truth.

He returned to the village not as a seeker, but as a knower. His presence changed without effort. His words were few, but powerful. He no longer needed admiration, he had awakened.

Unnai Arinthaal – If You Know Yourself...

There's a Tamil lyric that echoes through the soul:

"Unnai arinthaal, nee unnai arinthaal... ulagathil poraadalaam."

"If you know yourself, truly know yourself, you can thrive in this world."

Years ago, I didn't understand the meaning. But I heard it over and over. It echoed in my father's voice, hummed through his ringtone, and found a place in my subconscious.

Only now do I understand, those words were a **prophecy**. A seed of awakening planted long before I was ready.

This is your seed. This is your call.

The time has come to stop living from fear and step into full soul expression.

You are not broken. You are not too late.

You are a masterpiece in remembering.

The Soul, The Subtle Body & The Sacred Energy of Intention

When the Soul Speaks Through Everything

There is a presence within you that knows.

It existed before your thoughts, before your memories, before your name. It watches the seasons change, the pain pass, the victories rise and fall. It feels deeper than the body, hears more than the ears, and sees what the eyes cannot. That is the Soul.

And here's the truth the world forgets to tell you:

You don't just have a Soul.

You are the Soul.

You are not a body trying to be spiritual. You are a spirit living temporarily in a body, learning, evolving, and remembering your divinity through every experience.

But this Soul doesn't live alone. It is surrounded by echoes of energy, subtle frequencies that you've felt since childhood.

You might remember talking to your toys, giving them names, believing they could feel your joy and your pain. And perhaps, they did. Not because they had minds, but because they became containers for your love. You created bonds with even the non-living, your favorite pillow, your childhood cupboard, the tree outside your home. You humanized the universe, and in doing so, you built a sacred relationship with existence itself.

That wasn't imagination. That was intuition.

A child knows something we adults forget:

Everything around you carries energy. Everything listens.

Even if it doesn't understand, your intention is understood by the universe.

Speak to the stars. Whisper to the wind. Touch the walls of your room with affection. Talk to your pain. Praise your water before you drink it. Thank your shoes. Hold your heart and say, "I see you."

Love isn't meant to be stored. It's meant to be shared, with people, with trees, with things, with all that is.

The more you offer love without needing anything in return, the more you realize:

The universe is not silent, it's been waiting to love you back.

The Language of Light: Chakras as Soul-Gates

Within this sacred vessel you call a body flows a river of invisible energy. This river has centers, wheels of light spinning through you, whispering secrets from your Soul into your human life. These are the Chakras.

Each one is a doorway.

Each one is a memory.

Each one holds a lesson you came to remember.

They are not found in your organs or on x-rays, but you've felt them:

That tightness in your chest when your heart breaks

That rush of power when you speak your truth

That warmth at the crown of your head during deep stillness

These aren't random. They are signs that your energy is speaking.

Your Chakras are the threads weaving your body to your Soul. They translate spiritual energy into human emotion, intuition, courage, and purpose. When you breathe consciously, meditate deeply, speak truthfully, forgive bravely, these gates open. Your Soul flows. And life flows with it.

The Soul Doesn't Wait, It Whispers

In silence, it calls.

In synchronicity, it guides.

In dreams, in music, in sudden knowing, it reaches you.

The more you listen, the clearer it becomes. The noise of the world fades. You stop chasing approval. You stop craving noise. You start feeling everything deeply, not to suffer, but to become aware.

And when awareness grows, power returns. You don't need to know everything, you only need to know yourself. And from there, everything aligns.

Purity of Heart: The Forgotten Power

There's a force stronger than strategy, faster than logic, more magnetic than charisma: Purity of Heart.

To walk with a pure heart does not mean being naïve or perfect. It means choosing to believe in light even when everything around you is dark.

It means thinking with hope, even when your mind offers you a thousand reasons to give up.

It means showing up with truth, even when lies would be easier.

A pure heart believes when no one else does. A pure heart keeps moving even with nothing but 0.0001% possibility in sight. That fraction of hope? That is divine math, and it's all the universe needs to perform a miracle.

The universe is not fooled by appearances.

It does not respond to tricks.

It responds to intention.

When your intentions are clean, your actions carry energy. And energy is louder than words. The trees feel it. The wind feels it. Your room feels it. The people around you, whether they understand you or not, feel it.

Your vibration doesn't lie.

And when your vibration is honest, kind, and fierce in its goodness,

the universe protects you.

The Power of True Intentions

People may not understand your language, your goals, or your journey. But they will always recognize your intention.

When your intention is pure, unyielding in its goodness, it has a fragrance. You don't need to convince anyone.

Your energy walks into the room before you do. And the universe begins to shape itself around your path, pushing away what isn't meant, and pulling toward you what is.

This is not magic.

It is alignment.

There is an ancient intelligence in the air around you. It responds to integrity.

It honors honesty.

It protects purity.

So do not harden. Do not bend to cruelty.

Even if the world misunderstands your silence, your kindness, your dreams, hold steady.

Your consistency in light will summon protection you never asked for.

Because when your heart is pure, your surroundings become sacred.

The World Around You Is Alive

You are not alone. You never have been.

The wind you feel, the objects you touch, the room you rest in, they are more alive than we've been taught to believe.

Energy isn't theory. It's intimacy.

And when you begin to walk through life seeing everything as alive, your life begins to respond.

So name your pain.

Talk to your dreams.

Hug your pillow.

Smile at your journal.

Speak your needs into your water.

Place your palms on your chest and say, "I'm here for you."

Everything listens. Everything holds you.

You are already surrounded by divine forces.

The Earth is on your side.

The universe watches how you love, and loves you right back.

You Are Protected, You Are Empowered

Your surroundings are not just physical. They are sacred.

They know when you give with pure love.

They respond when you serve from the heart.

And they reveal their magic when you trust that your fight is for something greater.

You are protected, not by walls, but by intention.

You are guided, not by control, but by connection.

You are strong, not by force, but by alignment with truth.

So do good, even when no one sees.

Love deep, even when it hurts.

Give freely, even when nothing is returned.

Because when you do this, you're not just being good.

You're becoming divine.

And the divine is never denied.

And So, The Awakening Begins…

You've heard the whisper. You've felt the spark. You've remembered the truth.

Now, the path ahead will reveal more signs. Signs that your Soul is rising. That your ego is loosening. That your purpose is unfolding.

In the next chapter, you will begin to recognize the symptoms of spiritual awakening, both beautiful and chaotic, as the universe begins to strip away what you are not, so you can fully become who you are.

The journey has begun.

Your Soul is speaking louder.

And the world is listening.

Let's walk into the fire, together.

2

Signs Of Spiritual Awakening

When the Soul Begins Speaking Loud

"The wound is the place where the Light enters you."
— Rumi

Awakening doesn't begin with a divine light pouring through your window. It doesn't announce itself with grand visions or a voice from the sky. Often, it begins quietly, with a dull ache, a sense of disconnection, or a sudden hollowness in things that once felt full.

One day, you just feel... off.

You go through the motions, but something's missing.

The laughter around you feels distant. The applause that once thrilled you now leaves you empty. The goals you chased no longer spark desire, and the people who once knew you can no longer reach the parts of you that are stirring awake.

This isn't depression. This is the Soul beginning to rise.

It starts with silence, a sacred kind of silence. The kind that lingers in the early hours of dawn, in the pause between breaths, in the questions you don't dare speak aloud:

"Why am I here?"

"Is this all there is?"

"Who am I... really?"

These aren't signs of weakness. They are spiritual invitations.

They are not confusion. They are clarity preparing to descend.

They are the gentle knock of your Higher Self, the eternal part of you that's been patiently waiting behind the noise of the world.

And once you begin to hear that whisper... life will never be the same again.

The Whisper Beneath the Noise

You may not know what's happening. You just know something has shifted. Your outer world begins to blur, while your inner world grows sharper. You walk into rooms and feel the energy before words are spoken. You begin to sense moods, truths, lies, not through logic, but through presence. Your dreams become strange, symbolic, alive. You start to notice the same number everywhere. You think of someone, and they call. You ask a question, and life answers in a song, a stranger's sentence, a book left open at the exact page you needed.

You feel things deeply. Too deeply. The pain of others becomes your own. The beauty of a leaf, a breeze, a sunrise brings you to tears. Your senses heighten. The world gets louder, but you crave quiet. You withdraw, not out of sadness, but to listen better. The need to be seen fades. The need to be **real** grows.

And perhaps most of all, you feel tired. Not just physically, but soul-tired. Tired of pretending. Tired of the mask. Tired of holding yourself together when inside, everything is rearranging. You want to stop running. You want to stop performing. You want to stop carrying stories that don't belong to you.

You are not broken.

You are **awakening**.

The Unmasking of the True Self

The sacred shedding of roles, identities, and stories that never belonged to you.

As you awaken, something magical begins: you meet your original self. Not the one polished by culture or praised by society. The **real** you. The one you were before you learned how to survive. The one who exists beneath every label, every scar, every mask. You don't become someone new, you *remember* who you've always been.

At first, this remembering feels like loss. You begin shedding identities like old skin. You look around and realize you no longer fit in places you once called home. Some friendships feel strained. Some habits feel suffocating. The roles you played start to feel like costumes you can no longer wear.

And in that shedding, there is grief. But underneath the grief, there is relief. You are lighter. You are quieter. You are more *you* than ever before.

You no longer crave attention. You crave authenticity.

You no longer chase noise. You crave meaning.

You no longer want to be understood. You want to be aligned.

The people around you may not understand your changes. Some may drift away. Some may resist your shift. That's okay. Awakening is not about pleasing others. It's about returning to the truth that *never needed approval to exist.*

The Fire That Burns to Purify

Facing the shadows not to destroy you, but to reveal your light.

The awakening journey is not gentle. At some point, you will walk through the fire.

It begins as discomfort. Then it becomes pain. Old wounds rise. Childhood memories you buried resurface. Your ego kicks and screams. The shame, the guilt, the fear, they all come to the surface. Not to punish you, but to be seen. To be healed. To be released.

This fire doesn't destroy. It **purifies**.

You begin to understand that healing is not about fixing what's wrong with you, it's about releasing what was never yours to carry. You stop blaming. You start forgiving. You begin to hold space for your pain instead of running from it. You start loving your shadows, not because they're beautiful, but because they've made you who you are.

You stop asking, *"Why me?"* and start asking, *"What is this teaching me?"*

You begin to see that your strength doesn't come from perfection. It comes from **presence**, from showing up to your own life fully, even when it's messy. Especially when it's messy.

When Purpose Replaces Performance

The heart's shift from wanting applause to wanting to serve.

And then, something shifts. Quietly. Unshakably.

You no longer want to conquer the world.

You want to contribute to it.

You want to serve, not to be praised, but because your soul aches to give.

The work you do becomes an offering.

The life you live becomes a prayer.

You no longer compete. You collaborate.

You no longer rush. You witness.

You no longer perform. You **embody**.

You begin to understand that power isn't loud. Power is rooted. Grounded. Soft like water, strong like truth. You begin to feel deeply connected, not to a religion, but to the sacredness in all things. You walk through the world as if every step matters. Because it does.

This is the return to your original wonder.

The Dark Night of the Soul – Breaking to Become

Just when you think you've arrived, the deepest night falls.

Everything goes quiet. You feel disconnected, directionless, emptied. It feels like God has gone silent. You question everything again.

Who am I?

What is the point of this?

Why do I feel abandoned?

But this night is sacred. It is not the end, it is the **deepest beginning**. *Your soul is dismantling everything false that still remains. Your ego resists, and that resistance is what creates the darkness.*

This is the womb of rebirth. And you are becoming.

Let yourself dissolve. Let yourself surrender. Let the identity fall away, so the truth can rise.

The Inner Kurukshetra

There is a moment every soul must face, the inner battlefield. A war between your past and your future. Between fear and truth. Between illusion and purpose.

You will feel outnumbered.

Your doubts will be loud.

Your fears will dress up like logic.

Your past will knock on the door and ask to be let back in.

But deep within you stands your Lord Krishna. Your divine charioteer. Not fighting for you, but **guiding you**. Silent. Certain. Eternal.

You are Arjuna, standing in the chariot of your life, knees shaking as you witness everything familiar on the other side of the battlefield. Family, comfort, old beliefs, parts of yourself that once defined you, all now stand between you and your dharma.

And yet, you're asked not to turn away, but to rise. Not to retreat into what was, but to step forward into what must be.

In this battlefield, the arrows are your thoughts. The wind is your doubt. The silence is your only refuge. But when your soul steadies your hand and whispers, "Pick up your bow," you know: this battle is holy.

And when you pick up your bow, not because you're fearless, but because your truth is worth the fight, you awaken into your full power. You realize:

I may be surrounded by doubt… but I will not betray my soul.

This is not motivation.

This is not ego.

This is **Awakening**.

The Unshakable Rising

There comes a moment in every life when the noise around you stops meaning what it used to. The chaos, the comparisons, the doubts, they no longer shake you the way they once did. You begin to notice a stillness within you that feels older than your fears, deeper than your pain. A knowing.

This is not the beginning of a new version of you.

It is the return of the **true you.**

You are no longer reacting to life.

You are responding, with clarity, with courage, with consciousness.

You are no longer letting your past dictate your presence. You're no longer imprisoned by other people's expectations. You've begun to pause before the trigger. Breathe before the storm. Speak from stillness instead of survival.

This is power, not the kind that dominates, but the kind that *liberates.*

You stop begging the universe for signs because you realize:

You are the sign.

You are the evidence that healing is possible.

That survival can evolve into purpose.

That the light doesn't always come from above, it can rise from within.

You are no longer asking, *"Will I be okay?"*

You are declaring, *"I am already enough."*

This is not positive thinking.

This is **truth remembering itself**.

You are no longer chasing wholeness in others. You no longer perform to earn your place at someone else's table. You now understand what Carl Jung meant when he said, *"Your vision will become clear only when you look into your own heart."*

And so you rise, not with a roar, but with reverence.

Your actions shift.

Not to **impress**, but to **express** the truth you now carry.

Not to **win**, but to **serve** the higher mission unfolding through you.

Not to **hustle**, but to **honor** the life force flowing in your veins.

You create from **overflow**, not from scarcity.

You give from **fullness**, not from guilt.

You speak, not to be heard, but because silence is no longer an option.

This is the sacred shift.

The transformation that's felt, not announced.

People don't know what changed, but they feel it when you enter the room.

You are no longer trying to "become" something.

You are now **revealing** what was always there, beneath the wounds, beyond the masks, behind the noise.

You become a living transmission of what it means to come home to yourself.

Your presence becomes medicine.

Your boundaries become prayer.

Your purpose becomes not what you do, but *who you are when you do it*.

And the world begins to notice, not because you spoke louder,

but because your energy now speaks for itself.

You are the quiet before the miracle.

The soft thunder of someone who has *nothing to prove* but *everything to give*.

This is the unshakable rising.

The moment you shift from seeking power

, to becoming it.

The Spark Within

A Soul Story Inspired by Vedic Wisdom

Long ago, in the sacred time before time, the gods gathered to decide where to hide the divine spark of creation.

This spark held the infinite, **consciousness, joy, peace, and power**. If a being were to discover it, they would remember who they truly were: not merely flesh and mind, but **pure awareness**, one with the cosmos.

But the gods feared that if man found it too easily, he would misuse it, seek to control others rather than liberate himself.

So, one god suggested, "Let us hide it in the highest mountains."

But they knew man would eventually scale the peaks.

Another said, "Hide it in the deepest oceans."

But they foresaw that he would dive into those depths, too.

"Then let's bury it in the stars," said another.

"No," replied the wise one. "He will soon fly."

Finally, the eldest among them, silent until now, spoke with calm certainty:

> "Hide it in the **only place he will never think to look**,
>
> **within his own heart.**"

And so, the divine spark was hidden.

Not behind the sky. Not beneath the earth.

But **right where he always carried it**, at the still center of his being.

Ages passed.

Man searched for meaning in books, in temples, in success, in lovers, in war, in wealth. He wandered across lifetimes, chasing joy, avoiding pain, forgetting and remembering in cycles.

And then, one day, something changed.

Not in the stars.

Not in the world.

But in a man sitting quietly, beneath a tree, or maybe just in his room, exhausted from the chase.

He did not strive. He did not pray for more.

He simply **stopped**, and listened.

In the silence, he heard it.

A pulse. A presence.

A whisper from within that said:

> *"You've been looking everywhere. But I was here all along."*

He wept, not from sorrow, but from the aching beauty of remembering.

The spark had never left. It had only been **forgotten**.

This is not just mythology.

This is not a metaphor reserved for saints and sages.

This is your story.

Your divine spark has always been within you.

Beneath the ego, the trauma, the roles, the striving.

It was there when you were born, and it will be there when you leave this world.

And the only thing you must do to find it,

is **return**.

Return to stillness.

Return to breath.

Return to the place within where you no longer have to be *anyone*, because you are already everything.

As the *Chandogya Upanishad* says:

> *"Tat Tvam Asi, Thou art That."*

You are not separate from the source.

You are the spark.

And the moment you sit still long enough to listen,

you will remember.

Not as a theory.

But as truth.

LIVE AWAKE
A Return to the Self

Awakening is not the end of the road. It is the moment you realize,

there was never a road.

Only layers of forgetting.

You don't awaken to something outside you.

You awaken **from** the illusion.

From the trance of "someday."

From the hypnosis of hustle.

From the storm of "not enough."

Awakening is not a destination.

It is a **return.**

A return to your breath.

A return to the presence you abandoned in your search for approval.

A return to the part of you that has never been afraid.

> *"The Self is not born, nor does it ever die. Unborn, eternal, changeless, it is not slain when the body is slain."* -
> **Bhagavad Gita, Chapter 2**

This Self is who you are.

The one who has always been watching. Quietly. Patiently.

Beneath every breakdown.

Behind every mask.

Before every achievement.

And now…

You've tasted that Self.

Maybe in a moment of stillness.

Maybe during heartbreak.

Maybe when the noise got so loud, you fell into silence.

But once you've touched it, you can never unfeel it.

You see the world differently now.

Not with your eyes, but with your awareness.

You no longer look for signs.

You are the sign.

You no longer chase purpose.

You carry it.

You don't run from the world, but you're no longer consumed by it.

The marketplace still calls you, but your soul no longer answers to its voice.

And yes, it will feel strange at times.

You'll walk among many, but feel alone.

You'll laugh less at noise, and more at the miracle of nothing.

You'll value moments over milestones.

Peace over popularity.

Presence over performance.

People might say you've changed.

You haven't.

You've returned.

If they call you strange, misunderstood, distant, let them.

Even the caterpillar has no idea what the wings are for.

And when the world doubts you,

When logic says, "It's over."

When fear says, "Go back."

But your soul, gentle, firm, whispers,

"Keep going…"

Listen.

That whisper is the voice of the Real.

It's the same voice that guided sages in the forests.

The same voice that whispered to Arjuna before the battle.

The same voice inside *you*, waiting to be trusted.

> *"Atman is the light that shines even in the darkest night, untouched by sorrow, untouched by death."*, **Upanishads**

To live awake is not to live perfectly.

It is to live **honestly**.

It is to choose presence over performance.

Truth over tradition.

Surrender over control.

You don't need more steps.

You need more stillness.

Not another breakthrough.

But a breakdown of all the layers that keep you from **Being**.

You have awakened.

Not to escape the world, but to walk through it, lit from within.

Now, live awake.

Every breath. Every step. Every word,

As if you remembered what you forgot.

As if you're finally home.

Because you are.

Living Awake in the Real World
How to Practice Awareness Beyond the Pages

Spiritual awakening is not just found in sacred texts or silent retreats, it's found in the heartbeat of ordinary moments. The challenge, however, is not to awaken once, but to **remain awake** while life continues to happen.

The real test of presence isn't how deeply you can meditate in the Himalayas, but how consciously you can breathe when your phone buzzes with bad news. It's how kindly you respond when someone criticizes you. It's the choice to pause, to observe, to respond, rather than react.

Living awake in the real world doesn't require dramatic shifts. It requires **micro-awakenings**, small, consistent moments where you return to yourself.

As James Clear puts it in *Atomic Habits*, "You do not rise to the level of your goals, you fall to the level of your systems." So let's build a simple system, small spiritual habits that keep you grounded in the now.

3 Simple Practices to Live Awake Daily

1. The 5-Second Stillness Rule

Before you respond, pause for five seconds.

Whether it's a conversation, a decision, or a craving, pause.

This breaks the unconscious loop. It gives the Higher Self a chance to speak before the ego rushes in. As Michael Singer says in *The Untethered Soul*, "You are the one who notices your thoughts. You are not the thoughts themselves."

Try this: Next time you're triggered, silently count, *5, 4, 3, 2, 1*, and then ask, "What would presence do?"

2. Breath-Check Anchor Points

Pick 3 trigger moments in your daily routine where you'll check in with your breath and body.

For example:

Before you check your phone in the morning

Before your first meal

As soon as you sit at your desk

At each anchor point, take **3 conscious breaths**. Breathe in with awareness. Breathe out and feel your body.

This rewires your nervous system. It reminds you that you're not here to survive the day, you're here to live it. Awake. Present. Free.

3. The Mirror Journal (Nightly Reset)

Before bed, ask yourself:

Where did I live awake today?

Where did I fall asleep again?

What can I let go of tonight?

This isn't a guilt ritual, it's a gentle course correction. Over time, this nightly reflection trains your inner observer. And when the observer is strong, the ego loses its grip.

Living Awake Is a Lifestyle

Awakening isn't something you achieve once, it's a practice you return to again and again. It's the way you stir your coffee. The way you listen to someone without needing to reply. The way you feel your feet on the ground before saying something important.

You don't need to change your life to live awake.

You just need to **show up fully to the life you already have.**

Contemplation:

Where in my life am I still asleep?

What am I holding onto that I was meant to release?

What does "being awake" look like for me, not as a concept, but as a way of being?

Affirmation:

I am no longer seeking the light. I am the light remembering itself.

3

Mindfulness & Present-Moment Awareness

"When you realize nothing is lacking, the whole world belongs to you."
– Lao Tzu

The Moment That Saved Me

If I could split into two, one version watching while the other stumbled, broke, healed, and rose, I would tell you this chapter *means everything*. Because in every invisible battle I have survived, **the present moment was the medicine that never failed**.

I wasn't always this aware.

I once treated life like a project plan: finish school → land the job → buy the house → find the partner. I scrolled timelines the way auditors scroll spreadsheets, looking for the deficit called "Why-not-me-yet?" The harder I compared, the more I fragmented. My mind became **a thousand scattered shards,** half lodged in yesterday's regrets, half trembling over tomorrow's what-ifs.

Then one ordinary afternoon, the noise reached critical mass. Something in me whispered, *"Pause. Breathe. Just be."* The room did not change; *I* did. In that thin sliver of stillness I met a power deeper than hustle: **Presence**.

This chapter is an invitation into that power, and into a freedom few people ever experience.

1. Faith Over Speed

The Compass Beats the Clock

There were days; long, disorienting days; when I felt I'd missed the invisible bus that everyone else had boarded.

I'd scroll through my feed, seeing curated success stories: promotions, weddings, dream trips, dream bodies, dream lives. I'd sprint harder. Work faster. Network wider. Sign up for more. Post more. Hustle more.

And yet, somehow, the finish line kept moving.

The moment I thought I'd caught up, another metric appeared. Another "should." Another "not yet." It was like chasing a train I never knew the schedule of. I was exhausted, not from failing, but from **never arriving**.

And then, one ordinary evening, sitting in the corner of a dim hostel room, somewhere between tired and numb, a sentence wrote itself in my Notes app:

> **"Seeds don't compare. They root."**

Those six words unlocked something ancient within me. I wasn't late. I was underground.

The Problem With Speed

Modern society worships speed. We glorify overnight success, six-figure launches, 90-day transformations. But speed is deceptive. It tells us that progress must be visible. That momentum must be constant. That value is measured by **how quickly you get there**, not by how deeply you arrive.

But **speed without direction is distraction**.

As James Clear says in *Atomic Habits*, "You do not rise to the level of your goals. You fall to the level of your systems." When we rush without reflection, we mistake activity for achievement. We confuse motion with meaning.

We start living on autopilot, getting better at running... but forgetting where we're going.

Direction Is Spiritual

Direction, on the other hand, is spiritual. It comes not from the external map, but from the **inner compass**.

The *Bhagavad Gita* reminds us:

> "It is better to live your own destiny imperfectly than to live an imitation of somebody else's life with perfection."

The right direction doesn't always look productive. Sometimes it looks like I'm slowing down. Sometimes it looks like starting over. Sometimes, the most radical step forward is... a **pause**.

That night in the hostel, when I wrote, "Seeds don't compare. They root," I wasn't trying to be wise. I was just tired of feeling broken. But that pause became sacred. Because in that moment of stillness, I heard something I hadn't heard in a long time: **My Self**.

It said:

> *"Stay here. You're becoming."*

Psychological Insight: Why We Rely on Speed

According to behavioral psychology, our brains crave certainty. Fast results give us dopamine. They make us feel in control. But the deepest transformations, emotional maturity, healing, spiritual growth, purpose, don't work on dopamine timelines. They work on **trust**.

Trust in a direction we cannot see. Trust in a self we haven't fully met yet. Trust in roots growing beneath the surface.

As Cal Newport explores in *Deep Work*, meaningful progress comes not from scattered motion but **intentional depth**. We've been taught to chase the urgent, not the important. But deep transformation is slow. Purpose is not a notification. It is a **becoming**.

The Myth of Being "Behind"

The idea that you're "behind" is an illusion created by the ego and fueled by comparison.

Jay Shetty writes in *Think Like a Monk*, "We're not all meant to follow the same path. The only map that matters is the one that leads you to your own truth."

No two trees bloom at the same time. No two stars shine in the same rhythm. To compare your pace with someone else's is to **dishonor your soul's curriculum**.

You are not behind. You are on time for your life.

Let that sink in.

The Wisdom of Seasons

Nature never rushes, and yet everything gets done.

Spring is for blooming. Summer is for sustaining. Autumn is for shedding. Winter is for resting.

When you're in the winter of your life, you may not see visible growth, but that doesn't mean you're not growing. As author Katherine May writes in *Wintering*, "Plants and trees lie dormant. This is not their death. It is their restoration."

Faith over speed means honoring your current season.

Even when the world says hurry, **you must learn to listen to your own weather**.

The Compass Within

We all have an inner compass, a quiet, knowing presence that doesn't scream, doesn't panic, but **just knows**. Michael A. Singer calls it "the seat of awareness."

This compass won't always give you answers. Sometimes, it will only give you a whisper. A tug. A feeling.

"Go here."

"Call her."

"Let this go."

"Wait."

The compass may not speak in words. But it always speaks in **peace**.

To follow it requires surrender. And courage. Because sometimes it will lead you away from what's familiar. From the crowds. From the timelines. From the applause.

But it will always lead you home.

Learning to Trust the Pace

Faith is not passive waiting, it's *active trust*.

It's planting the seed and watering it even when nothing breaks through the soil.

It's choosing quality over quantity.

Depth over display.

Being over doing.

Here's what I've learned:

A slow "yes" rooted in alignment is better than a quick "yes" born of fear.

One step in the right direction is worth more than a thousand in the wrong one.

Presence is the antidote to panic.

You are not running out of time. You are unfolding *in divine time*.

What You Can Do Now: A Practice of Direction

Daily Compass Check

Every morning or evening, ask yourself:

1. "What direction feels right, not based on fear or pressure, but peace?"

2. "What seed am I planting today?"

3. "Am I rushing because of fear, or moving because of faith?"

You don't need to plan the whole forest. You just need to **plant today's tree**.

2. • What the Present Moment Gives

The present moment is often overlooked because it arrives so quietly. It doesn't demand attention the way urgency does. It doesn't scream like deadlines or glow like notifications. But when we finally pause, when we come home now, it gives us more than we ever thought we were missing.

Power, not as status but as clarity.

In the stillness of now, power is redefined. It's not about dominance or control, it's about **seeing clearly**. No distortion from past regrets. No fog of future fears. Just the truth of *what is*. When we are present, we stop reacting and start responding. We stop chasing validation and start creating with intention. That's real power.

Guidance, intuition louder than fear.

When your mind isn't echoing old wounds or obsessing over imagined disasters, something magical happens: **your intuition rises to the surface**. That quiet knowing. That gut feeling. That deep inner voice that never steers wrong. In presence, it becomes louder than fear, clearer than logic, and more trustworthy than comparison.

Trust, thoughts seen, emotions felt, chaos witnessed, choice reclaimed.

Presence doesn't mean you stop thinking or feeling. It means you **observe without drowning**. You see your thoughts as clouds, not commands. You feel your emotions without becoming them. Even amidst chaos, you reclaim your ability to choose. You trust that you can hold the moment, not escape it.

This is the most powerful version of you.

Not because you've mastered everything,

But because you've finally arrived, **here**. And here is where all transformation begins.

3. • FREEDOM: The Inner Frontier

When most people speak of freedom, they imagine an unstructured life: waking up when they want, doing what they want, answering to no one. But sages throughout history, from the *Upanishads* to modern philosophers, warn us: that version of freedom is an illusion.

That is not **freedom**, but *pseudo-freedom*, a life led not by conscious choice but by unconscious cravings, reactive emotions, and social conditioning.

True freedom is **not doing whatever you want**.

It's having the power to do **what is wise**, even when your desires pull you the other way.

It's not about escape from responsibility, it's about rising into it.

3.1 The Karma-Changer

Paramahansa Yogananda said it simply but profoundly:

> *"You are a free agent. Use willpower guided by wisdom, and you can change your karma."*

This means every moment holds the potential to **liberate you from your past**. Every mindful decision, every time you act with integrity, kindness, and purpose, breaks the momentum of old habits. You are no longer being *pushed* by past karma but **pulling yourself forward** through awakened choice.

3.2 Why We Lose Freedom

We lose inner freedom the moment we stop questioning what drives us.

We become slaves to things that don't matter, likes, trends, titles, roles, even praise. The irony is that even our virtues, when clung to with ego, can become chains.

- **Attachment to non-essentials** keeps us distracted.

- **Customs and routines**, old or new, can become prisons when unexamined.

- **Unconscious needs**, for love, attention, security, start making our decisions for us. And that is not freedom. That is management by fear.

The **Unicist Ontology** puts it clearly:

> *People driven by need are not free; they are managed by circumstance.*

3.3 Inner Freedom vs. Pseudo-Freedom

Inner Freedom	Pseudo-Freedom
Acts are adapted to reality	Acts are adapted to personal desire
Guided by responsibility and values	Guided by ego and gratification

| Prices are paid consciously | Prices are denied or blamed |
| Grows in service and scarcity | Inflates in indulgence and survival |

True inner freedom is hard-won.

It grows **field by field**, in health, money, relationships, purpose.

In each, you must:

1. **Define the responsibility** you're ready to own (not as a burden, but as a right).

2. **Accept the price**, emotional, mental, spiritual, you will need to pay.

3. **Act anyway**, with wisdom guiding and willpower following.

That's how you reclaim your power, **not by removing limits**, but by choosing the limits that lead to expansion.

This is not about becoming *free from* the world.

It's about becoming *free within* the world.

And that... is the rarest kind of freedom.

4.•The Five-Sense Grounding Ritual

(Return-to-Now Exercise)

"Peace is not found in a perfect future; it is hidden in this breath."

The modern world has mastered distraction.

We can scroll endlessly through other people's lives, ideas, and dreams... while becoming a stranger to our own body, our own breath, our own presence.

But there is one ancient and sacred truth that still cuts through the noise:

The present moment is not a concept, it is an experience.

And the body is the bridge back to it.

This ritual is not a spiritual gimmick. It's neuroscience. It's Vedic wisdom. It's real.

When your mind is spinning into anxiety or weighed down by yesterday, your five senses can become **anchors** that pull you back to the only real ground you'll ever stand on: **now**.

Sight: "I see ___; I am here."

Start with your eyes open. Slowly look around the room or space you're in.

Choose **five things** you can see.

Don't just glance. **Observe.**

Notice how light rests on a surface.

How shadows form gentle curves or sharp angles.

The textures, the edges, the stillness.

Let your mind pause with each observation. And quietly affirm:

> "I see this… I am here."

Each object you see is proof: you are in this moment, not lost in yesterday or chasing tomorrow. You are right here, and the world is holding you gently in place.

Touch: "I feel ___; I am present."

Now shift your attention to **four things you can feel**.

Maybe it's the warmth of your clothes, the ground beneath your feet, the breeze against your face, the pulse in your fingertips.

Let the mind soften. Let the body speak.

Run your thumb against your palm. Touch your chest. Hold your hands together.

And whisper to yourself:

> "I feel this… I am present."

This is your body saying, *I'm still here with you. Let's stay a little longer.*

Hearing: "I hear ___; I am aware."

Close your eyes for a moment. Tune in.

Listen for **three distinct sounds**.

Perhaps a bird in the distance. The hum of a fan. The rhythm of your breath. Or maybe... silence. (Even silence is a sound when heard with awareness.)

Each sound is a gentle knock on the door of now. And as you receive it, say:

> "I hear this... I am aware."

Because awareness is freedom. The ability to witness, not just react.

To be still, even in motion.

Smell: "I smell ___; I am grounded."

Bring attention to your sense of smell.

What **two scents** do you notice?

It could be the subtle fragrance of the air, a familiar perfume, the scent of your skin, or perhaps the invisible trace of earth, wood, paper, or soap.

Breathe it in without judgment. Just let it anchor you.

> "I smell this... I am grounded."

Smell connects us deeply to memory, to instinct, to place. It reminds us we are animals, alive and rooted in this Earth, not lost in mental simulations.

Taste: "I taste ___; I am alive."

Finally, bring your focus to **one taste** in your mouth.

It could be the aftertaste of something you ate, a sip of water, your saliva, a breath of mint.

Let it linger. Don't rush it away.

Acknowledge this flavor as if it were your very first meal.

> "I taste this… I am alive."

That's what presence does. It brings you back to the truth:

Not everything needs to be perfect for you to be **gratefully alive**.

Close the Ritual:

Place your hand gently over your heart. Breathe in, slow, deep, honest.

And ask yourself:

> "Am I here now?"

> "What is this moment trying to show me?"

Don't rush the answer. Let the silence answer.

Because sometimes it's not the moment that is missing you.

It's you who has been missing the moment.

Journal :

Write these down after the ritual:

- *What did I notice during the five-sense ritual?*
- *What surprised me about slowing down?*
- *What would life feel like if I lived more moments like this?*

You may be surprised by what comes up.

Often, presence opens the door to quiet gratitude, the kind that doesn't arrive through achievement, but through awareness. You'll notice things you hadn't seen in weeks: the softness of the light. The strength of your breath. The fact that, despite everything, **you're still here**.

And that is enough.

5.•Mastering the Mind: The Sacred "No"

"Freedom isn't found in doing everything, it's found in choosing what not to do."

There is a kind of silence that isn't passive, it's powerful.

There is a kind of refusal that isn't resistance, it's **reclamation**.

And there comes a moment in every awakening journey where saying **"yes" to yourself** means learning to say **"no"** to the world.

Not as rebellion. Not out of anger. But as a sacred declaration of alignment.

The Sacred No

Saying "no" is one of the most spiritual acts you can perform.

It is not about withdrawal or isolation.

It is about **discernment**, a deep inner knowing that says,

"This does not nourish my path,"

"This dims my light,"

"This costs too much of my soul."

And so you gently refuse.

- Say no to **invitations that shrink you**, even if they come dressed in politeness.

- Say no to **news that numbs you**, even if the world insists you must stay informed.

- Say no to **habits that hollow you out**, even if they feel comforting in the short term.

Every "no" creates space.

Space for clarity. For focus. For real joy.

You don't grow by adding more.

You grow by subtracting what's not *you*.

Positive Non-Resistance: The Path of Overflow

Some think resistance is the way to prove strength.

But real power lies in **positive non-resistance**, in holding such strong inner peace that the world is transformed by your presence, not your protest.

> *"If you want to remove the drop of ink from a glass of milk, don't fight the ink, just pour fresh milk until the ink disappears."*

This is the way of **overflow**.

You don't have to attack darkness.

You just have to be so full of light, there's no room for anything else.

This is not naive idealism. This is the essence of *sattva* in yogic philosophy:

A state of inner purity, calmness, and wisdom that can influence the world **without force**.

- If someone insults you, don't absorb it, **transmute it**.

- If negativity surrounds you, don't shrink from it, **outshine it**.

- If ignorance provokes you, don't argue, **educate by example**.

This is **non-resistance in action**.

This is strength guided by love.

This is *ahimsa*, non-violence not just in action, but in thought.

Commanding the Self Before Completing the Self

Self-command precedes self-completion.

You cannot create a masterpiece if your brush moves at every gust of wind.

The mind is your tool, not your ruler.

When you begin to **discipline your attention**, **protect your energy**, and **choose your influences**, you start reclaiming your **creative power**.

The world will try to convince you that saying no is selfish.

But the most generous thing you can offer others is a **whole, healthy, undivided you**.

When to Say No (Some Life Anchors)

- When it pulls you **away from your core values**, say no.

- When it **robs you of energy** without renewal, say no.

- When it **requires you to betray your inner truth**, say no.

- When it keeps you in loops of **overconsumption, overthinking, and self-doubt**, say no.

And when you're unsure, pause. Breathe. Ask:

> *"Is this coming from love or from lack?"*

"Is this helping me become who I was born to be?"

Sacred No Journal

- What are **three things** in your life right now you're saying "yes" to, but know in your heart are a "no"?

- What would change if you honored your sacred no with grace, not guilt?

- What could your life look like if you stopped managing everyone else's expectations and started managing your own alignment?

Closing Reflection: Strength in Stillness

You don't have to be everywhere.

You don't have to agree with everyone.

You don't have to respond to everything.

You are not a machine.

You are a soul.

And you came here not just to perform, but to **evolve**.

So say no, not from fear, but from love.

Because every "no" whispered in alignment echoes as a cosmic "yes" to the life that's meant for you.

6.•Self-Hypnosis of Truth

"Repetition carves neural reality. Choose truth deliberately."

There are two worlds we live in.

The outer world, with its shifting headlines, weather, timelines, and expectations…

And the **inner world**, which quietly, invisibly shapes the way we experience the outer one.

What most people don't realize is this:

The outer world responds not to your effort alone, but to the **beliefs you carry beneath your effort**.

If you believe you're unlucky, unworthy, unsafe, your mind will bend everything it sees to prove it.

If you believe you are guided, guarded, and growing, your subconscious begins to help you *become that truth*.

This is not magic.

This is **mental architecture**.

And one of the most powerful ways to build it is through **self-hypnosis**.

The Science Beneath the Soul

Your subconscious is not philosophical.

It is literal. Mechanical. Childlike.

It takes repeated instruction as truth, especially in **alpha and theta states,** when your brain is most impressionable (right after waking and just before sleep).

In these quiet thresholds, your guard is down.

And this is when you must **plant truth like a seed.**

Not just any truth, **your soul's truth**.

The Practice: Choose One Mantra

It could be:

- "I am guided, guarded, and growing."
- "Everything I seek is already within me."
- "I walk in divine timing."
- "I am calm, I am clear, I am capable."
- "I am worthy of miracles."

Let it be **short, strong, sacred**.

Let it feel like a sentence your higher self would whisper through the fog.

Then, say it aloud or in a whisper, **every morning upon waking**, and **every night before sleep**, for two minutes.

Not rushed. Not robotic. But like a prayer.

Like a reminder. Like the soul speaking back to the body.

At first, it may feel untrue.

But **the mind doesn't know the difference between imagination and reality**, it knows what you **repeat with feeling**.

And what you repeat, you become.

Believe First. Evidence Follows.

You don't wait to believe after it happens.

You believe first, **and then it happens**.

That is not delusion.

That is the **mathematics of the soul**.

>   Faith + repetition = new identity

>   New identity + aligned action = new reality

Everything you now take for granted, your handwriting, your voice, your personality traits, was once formed by **repetitive programming**. Why not reclaim that power consciously?

The Formula for Self-Hypnosis: 5 Keys

1. **Choose a truth-statement.**

2. Keep it emotionally resonant. Avoid negatives. ("I am calm" not "I'm not anxious.")

3. **Repeat in alpha brainwave moments.**

4. Upon waking and before sleep are best. Also during meditation or even in a warm shower.

5. **Use breath and rhythm.**

6. Inhale. Whisper. Exhale. Whisper. Let it match your heartbeat.

7. **Visualize it.**

8. See yourself embodying the truth. Let it become a mini movie in your mind.

9. **Stay consistent.**

10. 21 days. No skipping. Every seed needs watering.

Example Ritual (Try This Tonight)

Before bed:

- Dim the lights.
- Sit on your bed.
- Place one hand on your chest, the other on your belly.
- Whisper: "I am guided, guarded, and growing."
- Say it slowly, with breath, for two full minutes.
- Imagine your future self nodding in quiet recognition.

Then, sleep.

Let the subconscious begin its work.

Self-Hypnosis Is Not Pretending

This is not pretending to be someone you're not.

This is **remembering who you've always been**, beneath fear, doubt, and conditioning.

Children do it naturally. They speak to themselves in possibility. They live as if they are the superhero.

You are still that child, just buried under timelines and "realism."

This practice isn't a hack. It's a **return**.

Closing Reflection: Speak Like God Is Listening

Words are spells.

Your mouth is a portal.

Every affirmation is a message not just to your subconscious, but to the universe itself.

So speak truth, **not as a reaction**, but as a reality you're willing to claim.

Because the moment you repeat something enough, you stop arguing with it.

And when the argument dies, the new self begins.

That is the quiet revolution of **self-hypnosis**.

And it's already working.

7.•Reflection & Integration

"Freedom favors the prepared mind. Presence is the birthplace of every miracle."

There comes a moment, quiet, trembling, luminous, when all the words you've read, the truths you've repeated, the rituals you've practiced must now return to one sacred place: **you**.

Because knowing is not enough.

You must now **feel it**.

You must now **live it**.

You must now let these words rearrange your bones, not just your bookshelf.

That's what this chapter is for.

Not for answers, but for *honest questions*.

Not for strategy, but for *soul integration*.

Because transformation doesn't happen when you learn more.

It happens when what you've learned **finally lands**, in the body, in the breath, in the now.

So slow down. Find a quiet corner. Open your journal. Or just close your eyes and ask yourself the questions that matter.

Self-Inquiry Prompts: Where Truth Meets You

> Write. Breathe. Decide. These are the doors to freedom.

1. Where in my life do I confuse speed with direction?

Where am I rushing not because it's right, but because I'm afraid to be still?

What if I trusted that right timing is divine timing?

2. Which attachment feels most like a chain?

Is it my need for approval? For certainty? For comfort? For being seen?

If I set that down, even briefly, what version of me would emerge?

3. What price am I ready to pay this week for one authentic step toward freedom?

Can I let go of one habit, one opinion, one distraction?

Can I sit with discomfort long enough for it to show me my power?

4. Who, or what, needs my most loving, strongest "No"?

What no will make space for the deeper yes I've been avoiding?

What part of me is ready to be protected by boundaries instead of burned by people-pleasing?

Closing Blessing: Trust the Light You Have

"If your thoughts race, if your heart aches for more, pause. Close your eyes. Breathe. Whisper:

'I do not need the path to be clear. I only need to walk in the light I have.'"

That light may feel like a flicker.

But even the smallest spark can ignite a new universe.

You don't need a five-year plan.

You don't need to be healed, whole, or enlightened.

You just need to honor the light in you, **the part that already knows**.

That gentle inner compass that doesn't shout but **always points home**.

And here's what that compass says:

- Trust yourself more than the noise.
- Choose stillness before strategy.
- Let presence be the revolution.
- Let your "yes" be sacred.
- Let your "no" be holy.
- And above all, **remember who you were before the world told you to prove anything.**

Because **that version of you**, quiet, certain, free, is still here.

It never left.

Integration Practice: The Mirror Meditation

Tonight, or whenever the noise gets loud:

- Sit before a mirror. No makeup. No distractions. Just you.
- Look into your eyes. Don't flinch. Don't overthink.
- Breathe slowly and ask:
- "Who am I beneath all doing?"
- "What do I already know that I'm afraid to live?"
- "What part of me has always been free?"
- Then whisper your new truth. The one that has been trying to come alive through you.
- Say it aloud, even if your voice shakes.

Close with your hand on your heart and say,

> *"I am home. I am whole. I am free."*

Final Reflection: You're Already Becoming

Freedom is not something you win.

It's something you **remember**.

It's the moment you realize you don't have to chase peace anymore.

You only need to **stop running from yourself**.

So pause. Be here. Let the light in.

This isn't the end.

It's the **beginning of you,** finally, fully, freely.

Stay.

Breathe.

Become.

You belong to this moment, therefore the whole world already belongs to you.

4

Remembering Who You Are

"The Art of Inner Knowing in a Noisy World"

The Grand Illusion

Who You Think You Are Isn't Who You Are

> "You are not the voice in your head. You are the one who is aware of it."
>
> , *Michael A. Singer, The Untethered Soul*

There comes a moment, often quiet, sometimes painful, when everything you thought defined you begins to feel false. The career. The name. The applause. Even the struggles. They start to feel like a costume you've worn for so long that you forgot who was underneath.

We all play roles.

The achiever. The dreamer. The survivor. The rebel. The one who's strong for others.

But what happens when the show ends, when the mask slips, and you're left alone with the silence?

Who are you then?

This is not a philosophical question.

This is the question.

It is the beginning of awakening.

The False Self: A Master of Disguise

Osho called life a **"cosmic joke."** Not to diminish its beauty, but to remind us of its strange theater: how we spend decades building a version of ourselves meant to impress people we barely know, only to realize it was never real.

In *The Power of Now*, Eckhart Tolle wrote:

> "The ego is no more than a bundle of thoughts and emotions that you identify with."

Think of that. The ego isn't who you are. It's who you **think** you are, your history, your wounds, your victories, your failures, all woven into a script you carry like a passport to the world.

But the real you is **prior to the story**. It's not the actor.

It's the screen behind the movie.

Sri Ramana Maharshi taught:

> "The question 'Who am I?' will destroy all other questions. Until the questioner himself disappears and only Self remains."

You Are Not Your Name

Jim Carrey once said:

> "I needed to let go of the idea of Jim Carrey. That character was just a role I was playing."

That's not just a celebrity having a crisis. That's the core of every mystical path.

You are not your name.

You are not your Instagram handle.

You are not your trauma.

You are not your degree, your age, your job title.

You are the awareness behind all of that.

And the more you start observing your identity rather than defending it, the more you see:

You've been hypnotized. Not by evil. But by culture. By conditioning. By the lie that you are only as good as your last performance.

The Illusion Is Convincing

The illusion of identity is incredibly seductive. Because it works, for a while.

- You feel a rush when you're praised.
- You feel control when you're achieving.

- You feel seen when people validate your opinions.

But then… the applause fades. The goalpost moves. The mirror cracks.

You chase more. You hustle harder.

But the truth is this: **you are not tired because you're broken. You're tired because you're playing a role your soul never agreed to.**

In *A New Earth*, Tolle calls this the pain-body: an identity built on suffering, constantly needing fuel, conflict, validation, fear, to stay alive.

But what happens when you stop feeding it?

Self-Inquiry: The Mirror of Truth

If you close your eyes right now and ask,

"Who am I, really?"

The first answers will be noise.

"I'm Vikash. I'm a designer. I'm someone trying to make it."

"I'm not enough. I'm too much. I'm afraid."

Keep going.

What is the "I" that knows all this?

Not what the mind **says**. But what the **awareness** sees.

In *I Am That*, Sri Nisargadatta Maharaj says:

> "You are not the body, not the mind. You are the light behind both."

He doesn't say *become* the light.

He says: **you already are**.

And yet… we forget.

The Great Remembering

This is why journaling, meditation, and self-inquiry aren't self-help routines.

They are **soul-rescue missions**.

Every breath you take in stillness.

Every journal entry that begins with "I don't know who I am anymore…"

Every tear that says "This isn't me."

That's not weakness.

That's remembering.

As *The Way of Integrity* by Martha Beck reveals: the greatest peace comes not from fixing who you are, but from **stopping the performance** and returning to your truth.

The Masks We Wear

Brené Brown, in *The Gifts of Imperfection*, urges us to drop the masks we wear to be liked, accepted, or safe.

> "Authenticity is the daily practice of letting go of who we think we're supposed to be and embracing who we are."

So ask yourself:

- What roles am I playing just to belong?
- What masks do I wear to seem perfect?
- When was the last time I was truly, unapologetically me?

Write it down.

Cry if you must.

And know this: every tear is a drop of illusion leaving your system.

Pain as a Portal

In *Man's Search for Meaning*, Viktor Frankl reminds us that meaning can be found even in suffering.

Why?

Because pain strips away the inessential.

It makes the illusion unbearable.

And in that discomfort, the soul speaks.

Michael Singer writes in *The Untethered Soul*:

> "You will not be free until you stop thinking that the mind is who you are."

Let that sink in.

Freedom is not becoming more.

It's believing **less**, about who you're not.

You Were Never Lost. Just Distracted.

Let go of the notion that you have to "find" yourself.

You are not missing.

You are just buried under roles, fears, and societal scripts.

Your real self is still there. Watching. Waiting. Whispering:

> "I am not your résumé. I am not your reputation. I am the light that sees through both."

Journal Points for Remembering

1. Who am I beneath all my roles and responsibilities?
2. What is one identity I cling to that no longer feels authentic?
3. What would I do differently if I didn't care about appearances or approval?
4. When do I feel most *me*?

Write without censorship. Let the truth reveal itself through the cracks.

Closing Blessing

> "The Self is like the sun. The clouds of mind may cover it, but it never ceases to shine."
>
> – Ramana Maharshi

You are not the actor. You are the awareness.

You are not the story. You are the silence between the lines.

Let the old roles fall.

Let the false self dissolve.

And remember,

You are not becoming anything.

You are returning to everything you already are.

The Fool Who Follows Discipline

There once was a fool who woke before dawn, not because he was wise, but because something inside him ached louder than his sleep.

He didn't know much. Not about life, not about truth. But he did know this: something had to change.

So he rose. Each day. With tired bones and a half-believing heart. While others laughed or turned over in bed, he showed up for his path. Not perfectly, not elegantly, but consistently. In silence. In sincerity.

His discipline was not born from pride.

It was born from longing.

The longing to remember something he'd once known, something he couldn't name but always felt, like a melody he'd heard in a dream but forgot upon waking.

And so, he walked.

Through storms of doubt, deserts of boredom, jungles of distraction. He followed the same rituals, writing in the morning, sitting in stillness at night, listening to the wind instead of the world.

Sometimes, he looked around and saw people sprinting, fast, loud, glittering. Achieving, performing, ascending.

He felt stupid.

But something deeper than his mind whispered:

"Be patient. Water the root, not the flower."

And so he did.

His hands shook when he meditated. His voice cracked when he spoke his truth. He stumbled through conversations. He forgot his worth on Mondays and remembered it on Thursdays. But still, he stayed.

Rumi once wrote:

> *"Try not to resist the changes that come your way. Instead, let life live through you."*

This fool? He didn't resist change. But he didn't chase it either.

He simply showed up. Every day.

And eventually, his foolishness turned into rhythm. His rhythm became devotion. His devotion became wisdom.

Not the kind of wisdom found in books or sermons, but the kind that comes from keeping a promise to your soul even when your mind calls you crazy.

There's a Zen saying:

> *"Before enlightenment, chop wood, carry water. After enlightenment, chop wood, carry water."*

The fool keeps chopping. He keeps carrying.

Not because he's chasing enlightenment, but because he understands now, **discipline is devotion in action.**

It is how we prove to life that we are ready.

But here's the truth no one tells you:

Even the disciplined fall. Often. Hard.

They lash out at people they love.

They binge-watch distractions.

They compare.

They judge.

They forget.

But the difference is, they return.

That's the fool's superpower.

Not perfection.

Return.

He returns to his breath, his pen, his presence.

And slowly, gently, that return becomes his redemption.

On days when everything feels chaotic, when your old habits scream louder than your new dreams, do this:

The Return Ritual

A Journal Practice for the Fool in All of Us

1. **Sit with your chaos.** Don't solve it. Just sit. No phone. No advice. No fixing.

2. **Ask: "What did I abandon today that I promised myself?"**

3. **Write it down. No shame. No filter. No self-scolding. Just the truth.**

4. **Now ask: "What lesson did today want to teach me?"**

5. Don't rush the answer. Breathe it out. Listen inward.

6. **Close your eyes. Place a hand on your heart. Whisper:**

7. *"I forgive the one who forgot. I honor the one who showed up. I will return now."*

8. **Then write one sentence only:**

9. _"Tomorrow, I will return to __."

Not to impress the world.

Not to win at life.

But to keep your sacred vow to your becoming.

Remember, it is not the brilliant who become whole.

It is the one who dares to show up, foolishly, faithfully, with a trembling heart and a willing hand.

So if you feel lost, good.

If you feel foolish, perfect.

If you feel like starting again, begin now.

Because the ones who walk blindly but with devotion…

they eventually arrive where the wise feared to go.

And when they do, they don't say, *"I knew the way."*

They simply smile and say, *"I kept walking."*

Pain, Pleasure, and the Voice in Between

"Where Suffering Speaks, the Soul Awakens"

There are moments in life when the soul doesn't whisper, it screams. Through heartbreak, betrayal, loneliness, confusion, loss. The mind panics, the heart cracks, and something deeper than logic begins to rise. Something ancient. Something sacred.

Pain.

Not the surface pain of inconvenience or irritation, but the kind that rearranges the furniture of your soul. The kind that demands stillness when all you want to do is run.

We've been taught to hate pain. To avoid it. To numb it. We swallow dopamine like candy, screens, applause, shopping carts full of distraction. We worship pleasure and condemn suffering, as if one is divine and the other, a curse. But look closer. Lean in.

Pain is not your enemy. It is your **initiation**.

It is your body and soul saying: *"Enough pretending. Let's begin."*

Kahlil Gibran wrote, *"Your joy is your sorrow unmasked."* Joy, in its deepest form, isn't the opposite of sorrow, it's born from it. You do not truly know light until you have walked through your own darkness and survived.

And when you do, joy is no longer excitement, it's reverence.

Pain is not weakness. It's a **badge of entry** into a life lived fully and consciously. To feel deeply is not a flaw. It is evidence that you are alive, awake, and present.

Great souls have always walked with pain. Jesus did not ascend from a mountaintop. He carried a cross. He was mocked, betrayed, abandoned, and still, He loved. He forgave. He surrendered not to defeat, but to destiny.

That surrender is power. That pain, holy.

Jesus didn't wear a golden crown. He wore thorns. He was not followed because of His strength alone, but because He chose **truth over comfort, purpose over applause, sacrifice over ease**. He was the embodiment of divine dignity in the face of suffering.

And still today, the world praises resilience, courage, faith, but forgets where those things are born.

They are not born in the good days.

They are born on the floor, in the dark, in the moment you have nothing left, and you say *yes* to life anyway.

Pain, when met with presence, becomes **honor**.

Michael Singer writes in *The Untethered Soul* that we are not our thoughts, not our emotions, not even our pain. We are the one who watches. The witness. The vast, open awareness beneath it all. Pain comes. Pain goes. But who are *you* beneath the waves?

That is the voice in between.

Sometimes it sounds like a critic. Sometimes like a child. Sometimes it's the echo of your parents or teachers or society. It's tempting to believe everything this voice says. "You're not enough." "You'll always fail." "Something's wrong with you." But the truth is, this voice is not God. It is not even wise. It is **conditioned**, by fear, by trauma, by repetition.

And you, you are not that voice. You are the one listening.

Eckhart Tolle calls this the great awakening, the moment you realize the noise in your head is not your identity. That suffering comes not from what happens, but from how the mind narrates it. When you watch your thoughts like clouds in the sky, they lose their power. You step back. You become spacious. Free.

You begin to choose.

Not react. Choose.

That's where pain becomes transformation. When you stop saying "Why is this happening to me?" and start asking, *"What is this trying to teach me?"*

This is the spiritual pivot. The holy shift. The moment pain becomes a portal.

Viktor Frankl, who survived the Holocaust, wrote that man can endure almost any how if he has a why. Suffering without meaning destroys. But suffering with meaning is sanctified.

Maybe your heartbreak showed you what you really deserve.

Maybe your failure introduced you to your true worth.

Maybe your loneliness taught you how to finally come home to yourself.

Pain isn't random. It's precise. It's the soul's scalpel, cutting only what's false.

And on the other side of that cut? **Freedom**.

There is something about suffering that strips away the illusion. You can't pretend anymore. You stop chasing, performing, proving. You sit. You breathe. You feel. You cry. And slowly… you remember.

Not something new. Something *ancient*. Something is always there.

You remember who you are.

This remembering is not always peaceful. Sometimes it's messy. Sometimes it's rage. Sometimes it's the kind of grief that takes your breath away. But it's also the moment you stop abandoning yourself. The moment you decide: *"No matter what, I'm staying."*

That's the voice in between. The inner charioteer. The higher self beneath the ego. The gentle presence whispering, *"Don't run. I've got you."*

It may take a thousand quiet nights, a hundred cracked journals, a dozen shattered illusions, but you'll hear it eventually. And when you do, your pain won't define you anymore. It will refine you.

In his book *The Power of Now*, Tolle says, "Accept, then act. Whatever the present moment contains, accept it as if you had chosen it." This is not passivity. This is **participation** with life at its most profound level.

Suffering ends when resistance ends. And resistance ends when you bow, not to your pain, but to the wisdom inside it.

The world teaches us to chase pleasure. But **pleasure cannot teach**. It can only distract. Pain is the real teacher, the one who stays late after class and makes you rewrite the lesson until your soul gets it.

Rumi said, "The wound is where the Light enters." He wasn't being poetic. He was being honest. You will never know your light until it's the only thing left in the dark.

So next time pain comes, don't numb it. Don't scroll it away. Don't rush to fix it.

Sit with it. Listen. Honor it.

And then ask:

"When was the last time pain pointed me toward the truth?"

Write it. Name it. Bless it.

That's how you reclaim your power.

You're not being punished. You're being prepared.

You're not falling apart. You're falling *in*.

And on the other side of this initiation… is the voice that never left you.

The one beneath the noise.

The one that still believes.

The one that knows:

You were never broken. You were becoming.

And the pain? It was the proof.

Depression, Doubt, and the Invitation to Remember

"Depression isn't darkness. It's the dimming of a light that wants your attention."

There is a silence in sorrow that speaks louder than any noise. A silence not of emptiness, but of buried truth, the kind you've ignored for too long. Depression is not just sadness. It's not laziness. It's not a weakness. It is the soul's whisper growing tired of being unheard.

We often misunderstand it. We label it a defect, an error, a storm to outrun. But depression is not a failure of the spirit. It is a summons. A sacred ache.

It says: *Stop running.*

It says: *Sit down and listen.*

Depression isn't the absence of life; it's the soul begging to live more truthfully. It's not the end. It's the pause. A dimming of all distractions, so you might finally notice the light within that flickers quietly, asking for your return.

Like a forest in winter, it looks like death on the surface, but underneath, a transformation brews. Roots deepen. Stillness does its work. Trees don't fear the cold; they yield to it, because they trust the spring will come. And so must you.

> "Depression is your avatar saying it's tired of the character you've been playing.", *Jim Carrey*

Those words cut deep because they're true. You are not broken. You're exhausted from being someone you're not.

Doubt arrives beside depression, like a shadow partner. But doubt too is a gift. Not the enemy of faith, but its ignition. Doubt is the doorway that forces us to choose: Will we believe in the false voices of fear, or will we meet ourselves again with tenderness?

This is the invitation: not to escape your sadness, but to sit beside it. Hold it. Ask it why it came.

What does your depression want to show you? What part of you has been buried beneath performance, pressure, and pretending? What dream have you abandoned? What version of yourself have you betrayed?

You don't heal by fixing, you heal by facing. Depression is not an illness to be cured. It is a message to be decoded. Its darkness isn't evil, it is the cocoon. And what emerges from it is not who you used to be, but who you were always meant to become.

When Jesus wept, he wept not because he lacked power, but because he embodied the fullness of humanity. His vulnerability was not weakness; it was divinity made real. In his silence, he trusted. In his surrender, he transformed.

That is your path, too.

To suffer consciously is to birth the sacred.

You are not alone in this valley. Saints have walked it. Poets have written from it. Revolutionaries have risen from it. And now it's your turn, not to run, but to rise.

So if today all you can do is breathe, then breathe.

If all you can do is whisper, "I'm still here," then whisper it with all your might.

Because this moment is not your defeat. It is your return.

Write. Rest. Reflect. And remember:

> "Depression isn't darkness. It's the dimming of a light that wants your attention."

So turn toward the dimming. Not to fix it, but to feel it. Not to analyze it, but to honor it.

And you will find that the light was never gone.

It was waiting, patiently, quietly, for you to come home.

The Inner Dialogue: Talking to Yourself with Sacred Honesty

We all talk to ourselves. Not because we're broken, but because we're human. Inside you lives a council: the wise elder, the scared child, the wounded lover, the bold dreamer, the doubting voice, and the quiet healer. Most days, they argue. Some days, they weep. But all they want is to be heard.

Sacred self-talk isn't a sign of madness, it's the beginning of inner peace. When you pause to listen to these parts instead of silencing them, you begin to understand the whole of you. Try this: the next time you're overwhelmed, close your eyes and imagine you're hosting a tea gathering inside your heart. Each part of you pulls up a chair. Let them speak. Don't judge. Don't fix. Just listen.

Say, "I'm here. I'm listening. You matter." That simple acknowledgment is medicine.

Because healing doesn't mean erasing your voices. It means letting them belong.

In this space of sacred honesty, clarity blooms. You'll find that even your fear has something wise to say. Even your anger holds a truth you've neglected. This is not fragmentation, it is integration.

And when all your inner voices are finally heard, your soul exhales.

The Breath and the Blank Page

It begins with breath, not to escape, but to arrive. Inhale deeply and ask yourself, *"Who am I today?"* Let the question rise like smoke, not to be answered but witnessed. Then exhale, gently, and pick up your pen.

Don't try to write something profound. Just begin. Write the first thing that comes, even if it's messy, ugly, confused, or tired. This isn't about making sense. It's about making contact. You're not writing to perform. You're writing to remember.

Each breath is a bridge between the inner world and the outer one. Each sentence is a mirror. What you write doesn't need to impress; it only needs to be honest. Maybe today you're afraid. Maybe today you're proud. Maybe you don't know what you feel at all, that's still a truth worth writing about.

The blank page doesn't judge. It listens. It welcomes the whole of you, the wise, the worried, the weary, the wild.

Let this become your ritual. Breathe. Ask. Write.

Because sometimes, the only way to hear your soul is to let the pen speak for it.

And in that quiet ink, your truest self remembers how to **return to presence**, to clarity, to soul, to the place within where you always belonged.

The Sacred Fool's Promise

"I don't know where this path leads. But I trust the one walking it."

Maybe you won't find all the answers tonight. Maybe your journal feels empty, your breath scattered, your mind noisy. That's okay.

Because there is something far holier than having it all figured out: **the courage to keep showing up anyway.**

Every time you sit with yourself, not to fix, not to perform, but simply to *be*, you are doing something rare in this world. You are refusing the numbing, the rushing, the pretending. You are choosing intimacy with your own soul.

This chapter was never about becoming perfect. It was about becoming present.

You, dear reader, are the sacred fool. The one brave enough to walk into the unknown without guarantees, but with an open heart. You've stopped waiting for permission. You've stopped waiting for certainty. You've begun.

And that beginning, messy, trembling, unglamorous, is sacred.

Each breath you take is a vow. Each blank page is a portal. Each doubt, a threshold. And each quiet return to yourself whispers a single, quiet truth:

You don't have to know the entire path.

You only have to trust the light you carry.

You are already walking it.

And you are already home.

5

Nature Connection & Silence

"Roots Before Wings"

You don't need a mountaintop monastery to find peace. You don't need a thousand-dollar retreat or a guru chanting under the stars. Sometimes peace begins with something so simple, so ordinary, we miss it:

A single seed.

A silent moment.

A patch of sky.

We forget this in the noise of modern life. Screens glow brighter than the sun. Notifications ring louder than birdsong. And the mind, oh, the mind, is always rushing somewhere, chasing a future, rewriting a past.

But nature, in her ancient wisdom, invites you into another rhythm.

Not one of urgency, but of unfolding.

Not one of performance, but of presence.

There's something profoundly healing about watching a plant grow. You don't rush it. You don't pull on its leaves to make it bloom faster. You water it. You care for it. You wait. And in that waiting, something magical happens, *you slow down too.*

You sync.

You root.

The Psychology of Growth

It's not just spiritual, it's scientific. When you grow something, your brain responds with a chemical message: "This matters."

That's dopamine, the molecule of motivation, joy, and reward. It lights up not when you achieve the *end*, but when you're involved in the *process*. Watering a seed. Watching a bud bloom. Noticing the first tiny leaf unfurl.

Psychologists have discovered this again and again, that being connected to nature, or even just having a houseplant in your room, reduces anxiety, lowers blood pressure, improves mood, and boosts creativity.

You don't need a garden.

Start with a pot.

Place it by the window. Watch how it leans toward the light, how instinctively, it reaches for life. There's a lesson in that. No matter how confined the space, life seeks the light.

So do you.

Silence: Nature's Native Language

When you sit in nature, really sit, something strange happens. At first, the noise inside grows louder. Your to-do lists scream. Your worries throb. Your phone twitches in your pocket.

But if you stay, *really stay*, that noise begins to soften. Slowly. Like sediment in a stirred glass of water, the mind settles. The breath deepens. The eyes begin to *see* again.

Not through the filter of urgency, but wonder.

A leaf becomes a masterpiece. A breeze becomes a lullaby. Time stretches and something ancient stirs, a memory not of the mind, but of the soul.

This is silence. Not the absence of sound, but the presence of *self*.

The Sky as a Mentor

Whenever I plan my future, and I mean *really plan*, I don't sit in a dark room hunched over a laptop. I go outside.

I seek open skies. I stare at horizons. Because when my eyes see far, my mind begins to *dream* far.

You can try this. Next time you feel stuck, in ideas, in emotion, in purpose, go to a terrace, a park, a hill. Even a rooftop will do. Let your eyes stretch. Then ask yourself:

"What's possible?"

Don't force an answer. Just breathe it in. Let the sky respond in time.

But when it's time to act, to build the dream, brick by brick, then I close in. I go into the cave. Eliminate distraction. Get to work.

This is the sacred cycle:

Wide eyes to dream. Closed doors to do.

Grow Something That Grows You

Here's your sacred practice from this chapter. It's deceptively simple.

Plant something.

Yes, literally. Choose a plant you feel drawn to. Learn its needs. Name it. Speak to it. Watch it.

Each day, it will teach you something:

- Patience.
- Consistency.
- Grace in imperfection.

When it droops, care for it. When it blooms, rejoice. Let it become your metaphor. Because this plant isn't just alive, it's a mirror.

When it grows, so do you.

Rituals for Returning to Earth

- Sit in silence beside a tree. Let your spine mirror its stillness.

- Walk barefoot on grass and say, "I belong."

- Watch the sunset and practice gratitude, not for things, but for *awareness*.

- Every morning, open your window and whisper: "Thank you, life."

When You Can't Go Outside... Go Inside

Not everyone has a garden. Some don't have a balcony or a park nearby. But remember: *Nature lives in you too.*

Close your eyes. Feel the breath, the most ancient rhythm. The inhale, like a tide. The exhale, like a leaf falling.

This too is nature.

Final Whisper

You don't need more apps. Or hacks. Or life overhauls.

You need the sky.

You need soil.

You need stillness.

Because silence is not emptiness, it's full of answers. And nature is not a retreat, it's your original home.

So plant something. Sit still. Look up. Listen.

There's wisdom in the wind, a rhythm in the roots, and a light that never left you.

And if you listen closely, if you're very, very still, you'll hear the whisper in the leaves:

> "You were never separate. You just forgot."

Welcome back.

6
Gratitude & Positive Affirmations

"Gratitude is the wine for the soul. Go on. Get drunk."
— *Rumi*

Most people think of gratitude as a reaction.

Something nice happens, you say thank you. You get a gift, you feel grateful. A friend shows up, the sun breaks through, the rain cools the air after a long day, you take a moment, smile, and think, "I'm lucky."

But that's just the surface. A spark. A breeze.

Real gratitude is not a reaction.

It's a **state of consciousness**.

A vibration. A frequency you *tune into*. A way of being that shifts your entire perception of life, even when nothing's going your way.

In truth, **gratitude is not about having more. It's about seeing clearer.**

The Two People on the Same Street

Imagine two people walking the same street.

The first walks fast. Their brows furrowed. Their mind racing: bills to pay, people to impress, dreams unfulfilled. They pass a garden blooming with flowers, they don't see it. They pass an old man offering a smile, they ignore it. They're looking at their phone, scrolling through the lives of others, tallying everything they *don't* have.

They are not in the street.

They are in their mind.

Now picture the second person. Same street. Same bills. Same chaos in the world.

But they walk slower. Their spine is relaxed. Their eyes are open. They breathe in the scent of jasmine from that same garden. They stop for a moment, look up, and whisper: "Thank you." Not for anything specific. Just for *this*, for being here, now, alive.

Same life.

Two realities.

What changed?

Gratitude.

The Scarcity Spell

We've been conditioned into a trance of scarcity.

Modern society whispers endlessly: *You don't have enough. You're not enough. You need more to matter.* Every scroll on social media becomes a silent checklist: *Look what they have. Look what you lack.*

It's a clever illusion. One designed to keep us hungry. Consuming. Performing. Chasing.

But the soul?

The soul doesn't run on scarcity.

The soul *blooms* in enoughness. It opens in the warm light of gratitude, not because everything is perfect, but because the present moment is finally allowed to be seen as sacred.

The truth is: **you could have everything, and still feel empty.**

Or, you could have very little, and still feel overflowing.

Because **gratitude isn't about what's in your hands. It's about what's in your heart.**

Gratitude is Neurochemical Alchemy

Let's get practical for a moment. This isn't just spiritual poetry, it's biological truth.

Studies show that when you *consciously* practice gratitude, your brain releases **dopamine** and **serotonin**, the same chemicals released during moments of joy, love, and achievement.

You're literally training your nervous system to shift from survival mode to peace mode.

Regular gratitude journaling has been shown to:

- Improve sleep quality
- Reduce anxiety and depression
- Increase motivation
- Strengthen immune function
- Build resilience against trauma

That's not magic.

That's science catching up to ancient wisdom.

Your ancestors may not have had fMRI machines, but they *knew*. Monks, mystics, sages, they all practiced daily gratitude not as a luxury, but as **mental hygiene**. As emotional alignment. As the only sane way to live in an unpredictable world.

The Vibration of "Thank You"

Let's go deeper.

There's something mystical about the words *thank you*. Something primal. Primordial.

You're not just saying it to a person. You're saying it to **Life itself**.

You're saying:

- *I am not owed this breath, yet it's here.*
- *I am not guaranteed tomorrow, yet I woke up.*

- *I have faced storms and somehow I'm still standing. For that, I bow.*

Gratitude doesn't make life easier.

It makes *you* softer.

And that softness? That's what allows miracles to enter.

A clenched fist can't receive.

But an open hand, an open heart, can hold worlds.

How I Learned This the Hard Way

There was a time when I had lost nearly everything. My plans had crumbled. My health was shaky. I woke up every morning with dread in my chest.

I thought I was being punished by the universe.

But one evening, I picked up a journal and just... tried.

I wrote down five things I was grateful for. They were tiny: a warm cup of chai, the smile of my mother, a breeze through the window, the roof above me, my beating heart.

And I cried.

Because those things had been there all along. I had just forgotten to notice.

That night changed me. Not externally. Not overnight.

But *internally*, I felt something begin to bloom.

And the more I wrote, the more I whispered *thank you*, the more I started noticing the grace hidden inside ordinary days.

That's when I realized:

Gratitude wasn't making life better.

It was making *me* better at life.

Gratitude and the Shift from Victim to Creator

Let's be honest, it's easy to be grateful when things are good.

But the real magic happens when you find gratitude even **in the midst of difficulty**.

When your plans fall apart, and you say, *"Thank you for redirecting me."*

When a relationship ends, and you whisper, *"Thank you for the clarity."*

When the world feels heavy, and you breathe, *"Thank you for the strength to carry it."*

That's not a delusion.

That's mastery.

That's the shift from **victim to creator**.

From *Why is this happening to me?* to *What is this teaching me?*

Gratitude rewires your perception.

It doesn't ignore the pain, it transforms it.

It's the alchemy of the soul.

Turning hardship into humility.

Delay into direction.

Loss into learning.

A Final Whisper: What If You Already Have Enough?

Before we chase the next big thing…

Before we rush to fix, to upgrade, to achieve…

Take one breath.

Look around your life.

Not at what's missing, but what's **already here**.

You have a heart still beating.

Eyes that read this sentence.

A mind that can reflect.

A soul that *wants to grow*.

What if that's already more than enough?

What if, just for today, you stopped striving…

...and started thanking?

Because the doorway to all transformation opens with a single, ancient phrase:

"Thank you."

And when you say it, not because life is perfect, but because you are finally present, the whole world begins to change.

Not from the outside.

But from the inside out.

Why Gratitude Works

There's a reason gratitude feels like liquid light, it literally lights up your brain. When you give thanks, you don't just say words. You *shift your wiring*. Walk with me through this neat alchemy.

You remember that warm kick you get when a compliment lands right? That low hum of reward? Gratitude does the same, only it's sustainable, deep, and life-affirming. Scientists have discovered that when you practice gratitude intentionally, through journaling, thanking someone, noting what's good, your **brain's reward centers** light up *exactly* the way they do when you accomplish something or receive a compliment.

But the good doesn't stop there. A recent meta-analysis of gratitude interventions found that those who incorporate gratitude into their lives have **6–8% lower anxiety and depression**, better mental well-being, and even **decreased markers of inflammation**. Imagine stress as a fire in your body, gratitude is the water that cools its edges.

What's happening under the skin? A beautiful dance of neurochemicals.

First, **dopamine and serotonin**, the brain's happiness messengers, respond to gratitude journaling almost like they do to pleasant memories or a small victory. These aren't fleeting thrills; they build **emotional resilience**, elevate mood, and strengthen motivation.

Then there's **oxytocin**, sometimes called the "love hormone." Expressing gratitude, especially to others, fires oxytocin pathways tied to social bonding, trust, and nurturing. This isn't just touch or sympathy. It's a biological bridge that connects you to your community even when you're physically isolated.

The synergy between dopamine and oxytocin can't be overstated. These chemicals actually *boost* each other, oxytocin amplifies dopamine release and vice versa. The result? A gentle, sustained state of **well-being**, connection, and joy.

But the magic goes deeper. Chronic stress wreaks havoc in our bodies, elevating cortisol, disrupting sleep, inflaming our cells. **Gratitude interrupts this cascade**. Studies show that people who write gratitude entries before bed sleep better, feel more rested, and perform better emotionally the next day. Their real-life bodies say, "This matters," and then calm the fight-or-flight machinery down.

No wonder gratitude is fast becoming **the gold standard in positive psychology**. Weekly journalists show benefits far into the future. Who we become is deeply shaped by deliberate praise, whether to ourselves, others, or life itself.

Let's dive deeper: consider **the ventromedial prefrontal cortex (vmPFC)**, a region that processes value, purpose, and generosity. Studies reveal that cultivating gratitude makes this area respond more when you give rather than receive. In essence, building gratitude rewires your brain to *prefer generosity over gain*, what scientists call "altruistic rewiring."

But what does this feel like?

It's the softness when you wake up to the chirp of a sparrow instead of an alarm.

It's the warmth of holding someone's hand, not because you need anything, but because you're simply *there*.

It's the calm after choosing thankfulness in the midst of frustration.

It's biological. It's real. It's holy.

And beautifully, gratitude doesn't demand grand things. It thrives in quiet moments. A warm bed. A breath. A sunrise. A shared smile. Just three lines in a journal. That's all. Robert Emmons and Martin Seligman's research confirms that **even writing down three gratitudes per week** leads to better sleep, improved mood, and a stronger immune system

Sure, there are days when gratitude feels impossible. But that's exactly when it matters most. In the face of pain and hardship, a whisper of thanks says, *"I'm still here. I'm still caring. I still choose presence."* That whisper becomes a roar. The brain learns: "I can be resourceful. I can heal. I can rise."

Let's close with three soulful truths science confirms:

- Gratitude is **neuroscience in kindness's clothing**.

- It **soothes stress**, boosts **mood**, and **fires connection**.

- It **rewrites your reward system**, you literally want to give more than receive.

When you open your heart to gratitude, you're not ignoring life's storms, you're **building a sanctuary inside them**.

Today, will you say thank you to your life?

Choose three small things. Write them with care. Feel the shift.

This is a revolution not of circumstance, but of *consciousness*. Because when gratitude becomes your lens, life changes, without your life needing to.

From Victim to Creator

There's a moment in every journey when the question shifts from *"Why is this happening to me?"* to *"What is this shaping in me?"*

That moment, subtle, powerful, often preceded by tears, is when the alchemy begins.

Because until then, most of us are trained to suffer from the inside out. We wear our wounds like identities. We believe pain is punishment. That the universe is against us. That we are cursed, forgotten, or simply unlucky. We spiral in the echo chamber of "Why me?"

But as **Lord Krishna** says in the *Bhagavad Gita*:

> "Suffering is only in the mind."

And in that one sentence, the illusion begins to crack.

Suffering isn't the external event, it's the *meaning* we attach to it. It's the *story* we repeat about what it means. It's the silent contract we've signed with victimhood, often without even realizing it.

But gratitude? Gratitude severs that contract.

It doesn't deny the pain, but it rewrites the script.

It shifts you from prisoner to poet. From pawn to participant. From victim to *creator*.

Because when you begin to say "thank you" for the storms that shook you, you also begin to see the *roots they strengthened* beneath you. Gratitude opens your inner eye to a truth most never see:

You weren't being punished.

You were being *prepared*.

The delay wasn't a denial.

It was divine *design*.

The heartbreak wasn't your fault.

It was your *awakening*.

Gratitude, when fully practiced, expands your perspective beyond the immediate. It zooms out. It shows you the entire canvas, not just the dark brushstroke you've been staring at.

It reminds you: the fire didn't destroy you. It forged you.

The loss didn't define you. It refined you.

And when you start living from that awareness, even a little, you stop asking life to be easier. Instead, you ask yourself to become *stronger, wiser, more awake.*

That's what creators do.

They use everything, joy and grief, gain and loss, praise and betrayal, as raw material.

Even their own brokenness becomes clay.

This is not toxic positivity. This is radical clarity.

Because gratitude is not pretending the hurt didn't happen. It's standing tall inside the pain and whispering, *"Still… I trust this is making me more."*

It's wiping your tears and still writing thank you in the dirt.

It's feeling afraid and still walking forward with open palms.

The psychology backs it. According to Dr. Robert Emmons, one of the world's leading scientific experts on gratitude, people who practice consistent gratitude have *significantly higher levels of emotional resilience.* They're not immune to pain, but they're better equipped to respond to it with agency instead of collapse. Their stories don't stop at the tragedy. They evolve. They continue. They transform.

Because that's what creators do: they *continue.*

Gratitude pulls you back into the pilot seat of your life. It doesn't guarantee a smooth flight, but it reminds you: *you're still holding the wheel.*

Even when everything falls apart, *you're still here*. Breathing. Alive. Capable of choosing again.

And that, right there, is the shift.

From "life is happening to me"

to

"life is happening *through* me."

And maybe that's what Lord Krishna meant when He said suffering is only in the mind. That it's not about what happens, but whether we identify with the happening, or with the one who *witnesses* it.

When you practice gratitude, you become that witness. Calm. Clear. Awake.

You become the fire, not the ashes.

The sculptor, not just the clay.

And with each "thank you," whispered in defiance of despair, you remind life:

I am not your victim.

I am your student.

I am your co-creator.

And I'm ready now… to rise.

Ancient Wisdom, Modern Proof

The human spirit has always known the secret: when everything is stripped away, gratitude remains the bridge back to wholeness.

This is not a new idea. It is ancient. Eternal. Woven through the breath of sages and the silence of seekers. And across time, from a prince under a tree, to a woman standing in ash, to a shipwrecked man in sandals, gratitude was the thread that stitched brokenness into beauty.

Let's begin under the Bodhi tree.

He was once a prince. Draped in silk, shielded from sorrow. Siddhartha Gautama, heir to luxury, heir to perfection. His father had built walls, real and imagined, to keep suffering out. But pain, as the universe reminds us, is not stopped by gates.

One day, Siddhartha stepped outside those golden walls and saw the *truth*.

An old man. A sick man. A corpse.

And something inside him cracked, not in fear, but in *awakening*.

He left it all. The palace. The power. Even his newborn child. He wandered barefoot through dust and silence, trying to outrun the question that pulsed inside him: *What is freedom?*

Years passed. He starved his body. Beat it into obedience. But the answer never came.

Then, one morning, weak and worn, he sat beneath a fig tree by the river. Not seeking power. Not chasing enlightenment. Just *sitting*.

And something simple happened.

He remembered a childhood moment, sitting beneath a rose-apple tree, watching the breeze dance through leaves. That moment was joy. Unforced. Undesired. Pure presence.

A thought rose, quiet as the dawn:

> "Maybe the path isn't through denial, but through balance."

He opened his eyes. The world hadn't changed, but *he* had.

A village girl approached and offered him milk-rice. He accepted. Not with ego. Not with guilt. But with *gratitude*. Not for the food, but for the *invitation to live again*.

That was the moment. Not thunder. Not fire. But a whisper of thanks from the heart of a man who had let go.

That night, under the Bodhi tree, he met every shadow of his mind. Fear. Temptation. Doubt. And he sat still.

He whispered into the darkness:

> "I am awake."

It wasn't just enlightenment. It was gratitude reborn. Presence realized. Life is accepted.

Gratitude, in that moment, was the *spark of awakening*.

Fast forward to Oregon. A modern world. Wi-Fi and wildfires.

Clara lost everything in a blaze. Her house, her clothes, her artwork, all swallowed by flame. All she had left was her dog, her car keys, and soot-stained skin.

The news crews came. Friends wept. But Clara?

She smiled.

> "I'm alive," she said. "That's enough to start over."

Each morning after the fire, she wrote five things she was grateful for, on napkins, receipts, paper scraps.

Some days, the list was simple:

"Coffee. My dog's tail wagged. Socks. A kind neighbor. Hope."

Some days, it was hard. She stared at the page, tears staining the ink. But she always wrote something.

A year later, Clara had rebuilt, not just her house, but *herself*. Not in grand gestures, but in daily grace.

When asked what saved her, she said:

> "Gratitude made sure I didn't lose myself in the loss."

And now let's step further back. To a dusty street in ancient Athens.

Zeno of Citium. A merchant. Proud. Ambitious. Until the sea swallowed his ship, and his fortune with it.

He arrived in Athens with nothing but grief and calloused hands. But in a twist of fate, he wandered into a small bookstore. Picked up a scroll on Socratic philosophy. And something stirred.

> "Where can I find men like this?" he asked the shopkeeper.

The man pointed outside. "There. At the Painted Porch."

Zeno went.

He sat. He listened. He learned.

Not about wealth. But about *virtue*. About *control*. About what it means to *live well, even when you've lost everything*.

From that shipwreck, **Stoicism** was born.

Zeno taught: you can't control what happens to you. But you can control how you *respond*.

That's gratitude. Not as feeling, but as discipline. As for clarity. As *freedom*.

He never got his ship back. But he gained a soul so steady, it would go on to shape emperors and thinkers for centuries.

Gratitude was not a soft, sentimental word to Zeno. It was the anchor that steadied him when the winds of fortune failed.

And this is the pattern, again and again:

When the external falls apart, the internal is invited to rise.

And it's gratitude, not certainty, not answers, that carries people across that bridge.

The Buddha.

Clara.

Zeno.

And maybe, you.

Because life *will* break you open.

Loss will come. Confusion will visit. Control will slip through your fingers like sand.

But what you grasp for next? That's what defines you.

Gratitude is the hand you extend, not because everything's perfect, but because *something inside you still wants to grow.*

It's what says, "This too, belongs."

"This pain, this mess, this season, I can use this."

"I will not waste the fire."

"I will shape it."

Ancient wisdom confirms it.

Modern science supports it.

But most importantly, your *life* proves it.

You are not here to suffer blindly.

You are here to *awaken gratefully*.

And from that awakening… to create something unshakeable.

The Shift: Gratitude Paired with Affirmations

There's a quiet miracle that happens when two inner forces meet:

Gratitude and Affirmation.

On their own, they are powerful. But when they work together, when the heart is open and the mind is listening, a deep inner rewiring begins.

Think of gratitude as the fertile soil. It softens your heart, slows your breath, anchors your nervous system into safety.

And affirmation? It's the seed. A new thought. A possibility. A whisper of who you *could* be, if you allowed yourself to believe.

Gratitude says:

> "Look at what already *is*."

Affirmation says:

> "Now imagine what's *still becoming*."

This is not wishful thinking. It's not spiritual fluff. It's biology. Neurology. Energy. The deepest parts of your cells are listening. And what you speak, especially when your heart is tuned to gratitude, becomes your body's blueprint.

The Body Believes You

Here's what science shows us: when you feel gratitude, your brain lights up. Dopamine and serotonin, the "feel-good" neurochemicals, begin to circulate. Your heart rate stabilizes. Stress hormones like cortisol decrease. And something incredible happens: the *cells of your body become more receptive*.

Now, in this open, receptive state, when you speak an affirmation, "I am healing," "I am safe," "I am enough", your body doesn't argue. It *absorbs* it.

Researchers at the HeartMath Institute have explored this for decades. They found that when the heart is in a state of coherence (peaceful rhythms), the body's systems synchronize. Your heart and brain begin to "talk" more clearly. You are more creative, focused, emotionally stable.

And in this heart-coherent state, affirmations sink deeper.

They don't just bounce around in your head like empty mantras.

They enter your cells. They rewire memory. They soften trauma.

They become instructions, gentle blueprints for your becoming.

Why Most Affirmations Fail (and How to Make Them Work)

You've probably heard affirmations before. Maybe you've stood in front of a mirror, whispered *I am powerful*, and felt... nothing.

That's normal.

Because for affirmations to work, they must be *felt*, not just spoken.

And this is where gratitude makes all the difference.

Gratitude shifts your nervous system into a place of *safety*.

And safety is the doorway to belief.

In a state of fear, your affirmations are like seeds on dry stone, they can't root. But in a state of gratitude, the soil is moist, warm, alive.

So before you affirm anything... **thank first.**

Start with your breath.

Thank the air that enters your lungs.

Thank your body, however imperfect, for carrying you this far.

Thank the moment, just as it is.

Then speak. Speak not with force, but with *faith*.

The Right Words, the Right Way

Here are some affirmations that hold power, especially when paired with gratitude:

- "I am healing."
- (Thank you, body, for continuing even when I didn't listen.)
- "I am enough."
- (Thank you, past self, for surviving when no one else saw your worth.)
- "I trust my journey."
- (Thank you, life, for guiding me, especially through what I didn't understand.)

- **"Everything I need is already within me."**
- (Thank you, soul, for never leaving.)
- **"I am allowed to take up space."**
- (Thank you, breath, for reminding me that my presence matters.)

Say them out loud. Whisper them. Write them on a mirror.

But above all, *feel them.*

Feel how they land in your chest. Notice which ones make you flinch.

That's where your healing lives.

The Science of Self-Talk and Cellular Memory

Dr. Bruce Lipton, a cellular biologist, explains in *The Biology of Belief* that our thoughts affect the energy fields around our cells. Each thought, especially when repeated, sends biochemical signals to the body, changing how genes express themselves.

In simple terms: **your thoughts tell your body how to be.**

And over time, repeated affirmations (especially when emotionally charged through gratitude) reshape your biology.

They affect heart rate, digestion, immune function, and hormone balance.

They strengthen neural pathways.

They become the new "default setting" of your subconscious.

This is not magic, it's repetition.

It's neuroplasticity.

It's **you deciding what kind of reality you want to live in.**

A Daily Ritual for the Shift

Every morning, before your phone, your emails, the world's noise,

1. Sit still.
2. Breathe.
3. Think of three things you're truly grateful for.
4. Let them soften your chest. Let them bring a smile.
5. Now say your affirmations, three of them, aloud, slowly.
6. Let each one be a gift. A promise. A remembering.

Do this for 21 days.

You'll see something change.

Not just in your mood.

Not just in your productivity.

But in how you walk into a room.

In how you hold your decisions.

In how you treat yourself when things go wrong.

Because this is the shift.

Gratitude opens the heart.

Affirmation rewires the mind.

Together, they awaken the soul.

And maybe that's what true power is:

Not force. Not control.

But alignment.

The heart aligned with the mind.

The soul aligned with the self.

And every cell in your body whispering back:

> "Yes. We believe you now."

Soulful Practices

We often think transformation is some grand event, a retreat in the mountains, a once-in-a-lifetime realization, a thunderclap of clarity. But the soul doesn't require drama.

It asks for rhythm.

Small rituals, repeated with sincerity, become sacred over time. They don't just *change* your mind, they *train* it. They soften your inner world like steady rain reshaping stone.

So here are four soulful practices, quiet and simple, but immensely powerful. Do them not for performance, but for presence.

1. Morning Gratitude & Affirmations

"Begin before the world begins."

Before your thumb scrolls. Before your nervous system is hijacked by pings, alerts, or timelines, start with yourself.

Each morning, sit with stillness, just for two minutes. Breathe in slowly through your nose and exhale through your mouth. Let the exhale settle your heart.

Now, speak, or write, **three things you're grateful for**.

Let them be small:

"The warmth of this bed."

"My lungs, still breathing."

"The silence before the noise."

Feel each one land in your body.

Now, say **three affirmations** aloud. Let your breath sync with the pace of your words.

> Inhale: "I am healing."
>
> Exhale: "I am safe."
>
> Inhale: "I trust myself."

Exhale: "I am enough."

Don't rush. Let each one echo. You're not just saying words, you're watering roots.

2. The Gratitude Letter

"Even if they never read it, your nervous system will."

Pick someone, alive or passed, known or distant, who shaped you. Maybe they hurt you and taught you strength. Maybe they helped you once when they didn't have to. Maybe it's your younger self, still raw from all they endured.

Write them a letter. Pour it out without filters. Gratitude, sorrow, forgiveness, love, whatever flows.

Even if you never send it, your brain and heart will register the shift. **Studies show** that writing a gratitude letter boosts happiness, enhances emotional regulation, and lights up the brain's empathy and reward centers.

This is neuro-alchemy: turning memory into medicine.

3. Contrast Visualization

"Same life. Different lens."

Close your eyes and imagine:

Day One, You wake up, immediately reach for your phone. You complain about your to-do list, the weather, the mirror. You rush, spill coffee, curse under your breath. Nothing feels enough.

Day Two, You wake up, pause. You stretch. You thank your body. You open the window and let the morning air kiss your skin. You speak kindly to yourself. Nothing outside has changed, but *you* have.

Now ask yourself:

> Which version of you would I rather walk through life with?

This is the power of perception. Gratitude doesn't change reality.

It *changes how reality feels.*

4. Mirror Mantra Practice

"When you meet your own eyes, you meet your soul."

Stand before a mirror. Not to inspect flaws, not to adjust your face, but to witness yourself.

Look into your eyes and speak, gently and clearly:

> "I am proud of you."
>
> "I forgive you."
>
> "I am enough."

The first time, it may feel silly. Or painful. Or both. You may cry. That's okay.

You are breaking through layers of shame and silence. You are speaking love into the very place where inner criticism used to live.

Over time, the mirror becomes less of a critic, and more of a companion. A witness to your becoming.

These practices are not chores. They are portals.

And they don't demand your perfection, only your presence.

Do them with devotion. Do them even on the hard days, *especially* on the hard days. Because when life feels overwhelming, it's not more doing that saves us.

It's *remembering*.

And these rituals help you do just that:

To remember who you are.

To remember what you've survived.

To remember how sacred your life still is.

Even now. Especially now.

Real-Life Stories

Clara in the Ashes

The fire came without warning. One minute, Clara was sipping tea on her porch. The next, she saw the sky turn to smoke.

By nightfall, her home, her books, her family photos, her journals, her kitchen spices, the sweater her mother knitted when she was fifteen, everything she had ever called "mine" was reduced to ash. All that remained was her dog, the clothes on her back, and a heavy silence.

Reporters came. Headlines read *"Local Woman Loses Everything in Wildfire."* Friends offered blankets and donations. Some cried for her. Some cried with her.

But Clara?

She smiled.

Not out of denial. Not because she didn't feel pain. But because, through the heat and the heartbreak, she discovered something the fire couldn't touch.

Gratitude.

"I still have breath," she told one reporter. "My dog is alive. And I now have the rare gift of beginning again."

The next morning, she bought a notebook. She wrote down five things she was grateful for. Not grand things, there were none. Just simple truths.

"Coffee. Clean socks. The sound of birds. A neighbor's smile. Hope."

She did this every morning. Through insurance paperwork. Through temporary shelters. Through uncertainty. Her gratitude journal became her compass, her anchor in the aftermath.

A year later, Clara had rebuilt, not just her home, but her life. She opened a small garden café with hand-painted signs that read: *"We Begin Again."*

When asked how she found the strength to rise, she said:

"I lost everything I owned. But gratitude made sure I didn't lose myself."

Zeno's Stoic Path

Nearly two thousand years earlier, on another continent, under another sky, a ship was sinking in the Aegean Sea.

Aboard it was a wealthy Phoenician merchant named Zeno. He had spent his life building his fortune, navigating trade winds and markets, stacking his identity upon silks, spices, and ships.

But that day, the sea didn't care. It devoured everything.

Zeno swam ashore in Greece, soaked, broke, bitter. He wandered the streets of Athens with salt still on his skin and grief lodged deep in his throat. All his wealth, gone. All his certainty, lost.

One afternoon, he stumbled into a dusty bookshop. With nothing left to barter, he asked for the cheapest scroll he could find.

It was a collection of Socratic teachings.

He read. And something inside him sparked, not hope, not yet, but recognition. These weren't just philosophies. They were life rafts. The idea that virtue, not possession, was the mark of a rich life. That peace wasn't in the marketplace, but in the mind.

He asked the shopkeeper where he could find men who lived like this.

The shopkeeper pointed to the Painted Porch, the *Stoa Poikilē*, where thinkers and seekers gathered.

Zeno sat and listened for days. Then months. Then years.

He rebuilt not a fleet, but a philosophy. Stoicism.

He taught that while you can't control what happens to you, you can master your response. That gratitude isn't soft, it's strength. That calm, discipline, and virtue are the only unshakable wealth.

Zeno never regained his ships. But he gained something greater:

Peace. Clarity. Purpose.

Two Different Lives. One Common Thread.

Clara and Zeno were separated by centuries, culture, and circumstance. But they walked the same inner path.

Loss shattered their outer worlds. But gratitude became their scaffolding.

Clara wrote her gratitude each day to keep from collapsing into despair. Zeno practiced Stoic principles to keep his mind steady in a world that had capsized.

Neither of them escaped suffering. But both of them *transformed it*.

That's what gratitude does, it doesn't erase the fire or calm the sea. But it helps you walk through the ruins with grace. It turns ashes into ink. It builds philosophies from broken boards.

In both of their lives, gratitude was not an afterthought. It was the blueprint.

And if it could guide a woman through wildfire…

If it could help a man birth an entire way of life from a shipwreck…

Then imagine what it might do for you, right now.

Even in the middle of your own mess, gratitude whispers:

> "Start with what's left. Start with what's real."

> "You are still here. And that is no small thing."

8. Deepening Practices

It starts with one sentence.

"I'm grateful for..."

That's how you begin. That's how your breath returns. That's how your life shifts, not by rearranging circumstances, but by reawakening attention.

But like all practices, the depth comes not from doing it once, but from doing it *differently*. Intentionally. Repeatedly. Layer by layer. With eyes that begin to see what most people miss.

This is where gratitude transforms from a "nice idea" into a sacred habit that reshapes the entire structure of your inner world.

Daily vs Weekly: The Frequency of Reverence

Some people write down their gratitudes daily. Others do it weekly. The truth is: both work, but they work *differently*.

Daily gratitude is like watering a plant each morning. It keeps the soil soft. It keeps your attention tuned. It helps your nervous system regulate gently, moment by moment. Even small entries, "my pillow," "sunlight on my skin," "that kind stranger at the bakery", rewire your brain to look for goodness. And when you look for it, you *find* it. That's the magic.

Neuroscience backs this: people who consistently write daily gratitudes show increased activity in the **medial prefrontal cortex**, the part of the brain associated with empathy, decision-making, and joy. Gratitude isn't just a feeling, it's a cognitive muscle. And daily reps make it stronger.

Weekly gratitude, however, works like reflection. A zoomed-out lens. Instead of micro-blessings, you begin to notice patterns. You recall the arc of your emotions, the growth across days, the people who returned to your orbit. Weekly journaling helps you notice the *storyline* of your life, not just the snapshots.

Some research suggests that while daily practice primes emotional tone, weekly practice deepens emotional *integration*. So you don't have to choose between them. Use both. Water the present. Nourish the past.

Thanking More Than Just "The Good Stuff"

Gratitude matures when you stop thanking only the obvious.

Start appreciating strangers.

The delivery guy who smiled even in the rain.

The woman in traffic who let you merge.

The barista who added whipped cream without charging extra.

Thank nature.

That one bird that always returns to your windowsill.

The tree that held its ground through last night's storm.

The wind that cooled your skin when no one else noticed.

Thank your **past self**.

The "you" who didn't quit when they had every reason to.

The "you" who kept breathing through heartbreak, confusion, self-doubt.

The "you" who still showed up.

This wide-field appreciation isn't just poetic, it's scientifically grounded.

A study published in *Social Cognitive and Affective Neuroscience* showed that expressing gratitude toward *non-social* elements (like nature, memories, even the *universe itself*) stimulates broader neural engagement than personal gratitude alone. It connects you to something larger than yourself.

Gratitude, in its purest form, says: *"I see."*

I see the grace in this chaos.

I see the beauty in this mess.

I see *me*, trying, and that is enough.

Affirmation as Anchor

Words change us.

Not just the ones spoken to us, but the ones we speak *to ourselves*.

Once you find the affirmations that resonate with your soul, **keep them close**. Not just in your journal, but on your lock screen. On sticky notes. In your wallet. On your mirror. On the inside of your planner. Tucked into a book. Memorized like prayers.

Here are a few soul-tested, body-approved lines that work like medicine:

- "I am safe here."
- "This moment is enough."
- "I am loved, even when I don't feel it."
- "My presence matters."
- "I don't have to be perfect to be powerful."
- "The universe hasn't forgotten me."

Each time you repeat them, say them not like you're convincing yourself, but like you're *reminding* yourself. Like the truth was always there, waiting beneath the noise.

Cellular biology suggests this isn't woo-woo, it's **epigenetics**.

Positive affirmations, especially when combined with emotional intensity (like gratitude), influence **gene expression**. Your words can quite literally instruct your cells how to behave, whether to inflame or heal, contract or expand.

So the next time you say "I am healing,"

Know that your body hears it.

Your breath adjusts.

Your nervous system listens.

And a ripple of biological agreement begins.

Gratitude is not a finish line. It's a rhythm. A ritual. A way of returning to presence even as the world spins. When you pair it with affirmations, with words charged with meaning, you become the artist of your own vibration.

So carry your practice like a compass. Let it whisper directions. Let it shift your gaze.

You won't always feel grateful.

But you can always return to it.

And when you do, life begins to respond in kind.

Final Reflection & Blessing

Take a breath.

Right now. Gently.

Notice the air filling your lungs, the miracle you didn't ask for, the life moving through you even when you forget to notice. This breath… is a blessing. Not earned. Not demanded. Just given. Freely. Lovingly.

And that alone means this:

You are already rich.

Maybe your life isn't where you thought it would be. Maybe you carry scars no one sees. Maybe your mind still whispers stories of lack, loneliness, fear.

But the fact that you're reading these words, that you've made it this far, means the story isn't over.

It means you still have the sacred power to choose. To return. To begin again.

Let today be that quiet beginning.

Let this moment be a soft hand on your back, reminding you: *You are not too late. You are not behind. You are not broken.*

You are breathing.

You are listening.

You are remembering what your soul has always known,

That the real treasure of life was never in perfection, or performance, or praise.

It was on pause.

Noticing.

The whisper of "thank you" in the middle of an ordinary day.

Gratitude is not something you chase.

It's something you wake up to.

So drink the wine of gratitude.

Let each "thank you" be a sip of the divine, poured not into a golden chalice, but into the open cup of your heart.

Thank you for your breath.

Thank you for the tears that taught you.

Thank you for the laughter that healed you.

Thank you for the strength you didn't know you had.

Thank you for still believing, even on days when it felt impossible.

Gratitude is the language of the soul.

And when you speak it, everything softens. The sharp edges inside you round into peace. The dark corners of the mind begin to glow.

You remember that no matter how much you've lost...

You've never lost yourself.

So hold yourself gently.

Forgive what you didn't know.

Bless what is becoming.

You are not your past.

You are not your pain.

You are the presence within it all, the one who sees, the one who stays, the one who says:

"I am still here. And I am thankful."

May your mornings begin with reverence.

May your nights end with grace.

May your words heal you.

May your thoughts guide you home.

And whenever doubt returns, as it will, simply return to this truth:

You are already whole.

You are already loved.

You are already enough.

And that?

That is something to be deeply, endlessly grateful for.

7

Healing The Past & Releasing Pain

"You cannot heal what you do not feel."

Each section has a purpose: to guide you from

wound → awareness → release → rebirth.

The Silent Weight of the Past

There are moments in life that pass, but never really leave.

They settle not as memories, but as **sensations**. A heaviness in the chest. A tightness in the throat. A subtle flinch when someone raises their voice. The inability to say no, even when everything inside screams to. These aren't random reactions. These are echoes, echoes of pain that was never fully felt. Never acknowledged. Never loved back into wholeness.

For the longest time, I believed I had moved on. I thought because I wasn't thinking about the past daily, it no longer had power over me. I told myself the lie most of us tell:

"I'm over it."

But healing doesn't mean forgetting, and it definitely doesn't mean ignoring.

Healing means having the **courage to feel what we once had to numb** in order to survive.

You see, the past rarely returns in neat, obvious ways. It doesn't knock on your door saying, *"Hey, remember me?"* It sneaks in quietly, disguised as behaviors.

It becomes **our patterns.**

It whispers through how we react, how we protect ourselves, how we love... or struggle to love.

When Behaviors Are Just Ghosts Wearing Masks

We've normalized dysfunction so deeply that we don't even realize we're carrying trauma. We call it "just how I am."

But look closer.

- **Perfectionism?** Often rooted in a fear of being criticized or rejected. Maybe you grew up in a home where love was conditional, based on performance or grades or obedience.

- **People-pleasing?** A deep fear of abandonment. Maybe the approval of others was your survival tool. Maybe you learned that being liked = being safe.

- **Rage?** Not evil. Just **unexpressed sadness**. Anger is often grief's first mask.

- **Control issues?** Almost always stem from **chaos in childhood**, where unpredictability felt like danger, and control became your safety blanket.

We don't become these things out of choice.

We become them out of *necessity*.

And that's where compassion must begin.

Because before you can heal a pattern, you must **first see it**. Not with shame, but with understanding.

Like a parent who finally notices their child acting out, not because they're bad… but because they've been hurting quietly for too long.

"I'm Not Overreacting, I'm Remembering."

Have you ever wondered why you feel disproportionately emotional in some situations?

Someone cancels plans, and suddenly you feel rejected, small, abandoned.

Your partner doesn't text back, and it triggers panic.

A colleague criticizes your work, and your chest tightens for the rest of the day.

These aren't just reactions to the present. They're **activations of the past**.

The nervous system doesn't tell time.

When something in the present resembles something painful from the past, even slightly, your body responds as if it's happening **all over again**.

That's not weakness.

That's unhealed pain saying, "Please see me now. Please free me."

Healing Begins with Seeing

Most people try to change their behavior without exploring the root of it. That's like chopping off the leaves of a weed while the root stays untouched.

Real transformation begins when you ask:

"Where did I first learn to be this way?"

"What was I trying to protect myself from?"

"What was the unspoken rule in my childhood, and how did it shape me?"

It's not about blaming your past. It's about **liberating your future**.

You are not broken.

You are patterned.

And patterns can be rewritten, once the pain beneath them is felt.

Exercise Box: The *Pattern to Pain* Map

Let's gently explore your most recurring emotional patterns. You don't have to force anything. Just stay curious.

Step 1: Identify the Pattern

What do you notice in yourself, especially under stress or in relationships?

Examples:

- I avoid conflict at all costs
- I always say yes even when I don't want to
- I need constant validation
- I'm scared of being alone
- I overwork myself and still feel "not enough"

Write it down.

Step 2: Trace It Back

Ask yourself:

- *"When did I first feel this way?"*
- *"Who did I have to become to feel safe or loved?"*
- *"What was I afraid would happen if I didn't behave this way?"*

Go back, not with judgment, but with compassion. Hold the younger version of you in your heart.

Step 3: Connect to the Emotion

What feeling is buried under this behavior?

- Fear
- Grief
- Shame
- Guilt
- Abandonment
- Loneliness

Allow yourself to feel it, just for a few seconds. Breathe through it. No need to fix it. Just **witness** it. That alone begins the release.

Step 4: Offer Understanding

Whisper to that part of you:

> "You were trying to stay safe. I see you. Thank you.
>
> But now I choose a new way."

A Quiet Truth

Healing doesn't always look like breakthroughs or tears.

Sometimes, it's in the quiet decision to pause before reacting.

To take a breath instead of defending.

To say "no" without guilt.

To stop chasing love that keeps wounding you.

To finally, gently, stop betraying yourself.

The weight of the past only stays when we refuse to look.

But when we do, when we meet our past not with fear but with love, something magical happens:

We stop being the story... and start becoming the author.

And that's when healing truly begins.

Revisiting the Younger Self

"Trauma isn't what happened to you. It's what you felt inside... and never got to express.", *Dr. Gabor Maté*

We all carry within us a child, not in memory, but in energy.

The 5-year-old who cried alone in a corner, not understanding why everyone was shouting.

The 10-year-old who pretended to be okay at school, even though things were falling apart at home.

The 15-year-old who looked in the mirror and hated what they saw, craving acceptance from a world that offered none.

They didn't disappear when you turned 18.

They didn't vanish after your degree, your job, your breakup, or your success.

They're still here, in the way your voice shakes when you say "no,"

In the way your body tenses when someone raises their voice,

In the way you sometimes feel small for no logical reason at all.

Your *inner child* is not a metaphor.

It's a very real, very alive part of your nervous system, still frozen in moments you never got to process.

Reparenting: Becoming Who You Needed

Most of us never had the space to fully feel, let alone heal.

We were told to "stop crying," "move on," "be strong."

But feelings don't vanish just because they're silenced.

They go underground.

They become beliefs.

They become patterns.

They become pain dressed up as personality.

As *Dr. Nicole LePera* writes, "You don't just grow out of childhood wounds, you grow around them."

That's why so many of us reach adulthood with achievements, followers, or relationships, and still feel hollow inside. Because no amount of external validation can heal an internal fracture.

The only way to repair that fracture is to **go back**.

Not to relive, but to *reparent*.

To meet those younger versions of yourself not with judgment or analysis… but with presence.

The Letter Ritual: Writing to the Past

One of the most powerful practices I ever did was writing letters to my younger selves.

I started with the five-year-old version of me, shy, sensitive, wide-eyed, wondering why the world felt so loud and unsafe.

Then the ten-year-old, eager to be seen, but already learning to dim their light.

Then the fifteen-year-old, battling shame, self-hate, confusion, longing, and feeling utterly alone in their own body.

And here's the most important part:

I didn't try to *fix* them.

I didn't try to give them lessons or advice.

I simply *witnessed* them.

Held space.

Loved them the way no one had loved them back then, fully, without conditions.

It felt awkward at first. I questioned it. But the moment I started writing, tears came I didn't even know were still inside me.

Because those younger selves?

They weren't just memories.

They were *waiting*.

Waiting to be seen.

Waiting to be heard.

Waiting for someone, anyone, to say:

> "It wasn't your fault."

> "You didn't deserve that."

> "I'm here now. And I'm not leaving."

That someone... was me.

The Mirror of Time (Ritual Practice)

If you're ready, here's something you can try.

Find a quiet space. Dim the lights. Sit in stillness. Put your hand on your heart. Breathe.

Then close your eyes, and imagine this:

A door opens... and in walks a younger version of *you*.

Maybe five. Maybe ten. Maybe fifteen. You don't choose, they do.

What do they look like?

What are they wearing?

What is the expression on their face?

What emotion are they carrying?

Don't force the scene. Just let it unfold.

Let them sit across from you.

Now, gently ask them:

> "What do you want me to know?"
>
> "What do you wish someone had told you back then?"
>
> "What do you need from me today?"

Then simply *listen*. Don't interrupt. Don't correct. Just witness.

You may hear nothing. Or you may hear everything, all at once.

A sob. A sentence. A silence.

Let it happen. Let your body feel. Let your heart break open if it needs to.

Then... when the time feels right... say to them:

> "I see you."
>
> "I love you."

"I promise to protect you now."

If you feel ready, open your arms, and imagine holding that younger self.

Let them cry. Let them rest. Let them merge into your heart.

Because that's where they've always belonged, *not abandoned in time*, but *welcomed home*.

The Psychology of Inner Child Work

According to *Gabor Maté*, trauma isn't the event itself, it's what happened **inside us** during the event.

It's the emotions we couldn't express. The confusion we had to swallow. The shame we carried silently.

Revisiting the inner child isn't about blaming anyone.

It's about reclaiming what was once buried: our wholeness.

Modern neuroscience backs this up.

When you emotionally "witness" yourself, especially during visualization or journaling, you're literally rewiring your brain.

The **prefrontal cortex** (logic and compassion) connects with the **amygdala** (fear center), and emotional memory starts to shift.

You don't erase the pain.

You simply **meet it with love**, and that alone changes everything.

Final Reflection

There's no brokenness in you, only parts of you that are tired of being left behind.

When you return to your younger self with gentleness, you don't regress.

You *rise*.

You rise by becoming the parent, the friend, the guardian, the protector that your inner child never had.

You rise by no longer needing someone else to heal you, because you're learning to heal yourself.

So tonight, if your heart aches, let it.

Write the letter. Open the door. Hold the child.

Tell them,

> "You didn't deserve the pain…
>
> But you absolutely deserve the peace."

And watch what happens when love travels back in time.

Because healing doesn't always begin in the present.

Sometimes, it begins in the past, when you finally go back for the child who was waiting to be seen.

The Saturn Archetype: Lessons in Disguise

"Time is a circle. What we do not face, returns again, dressed in new clothes, but carrying the same test."

There are some lessons in life that don't whisper, they thunder.

They don't arrive wrapped in love or clarity.

They arrive as loss. Delay. Illness. Rejection. Silence.

And yet, when you learn to look beyond their surface, you'll see a hidden face watching you quietly. Not punishing, but witnessing.

Not cruel, but unwavering.

That face is Saturn.

In astrology, Saturn isn't a villain. It's a gatekeeper.

The one who stands between your old life and your higher life and asks,

> "Have you truly grown? Are you ready for more?
> Or are you still hiding in your old patterns, pretending they don't exist?"

Saturn is not about punishment. It is about **accountability**.

It is the cosmic parent. The karmic examiner. The one force in the sky that doesn't care about your charm, your wishes, or your excuses.

It only watches your **actions**, your consistency, your responsibility, your effort.

And then it gives you exactly what you've earned. No more, no less.

This is the hardest kind of love.

But it is also the most *real*.

The Gaze of Shani: Justice, Not Cruelty

In Indian mythology, Shani Dev, the deity representing Saturn, is both revered and feared. He is the god of **karma**, the embodiment of cosmic justice. His gaze is said to bring hardship, not because he is evil, but because he reveals what is unhealed, what is misaligned, what is unsustainable.

When Shani's gaze falls upon you, it doesn't destroy. It **tests**.

And like gold tested in fire, the purpose is purification, not pain.

Legend tells us that even the gods could not escape his gaze.

Lord Shiva himself, the Mahadeva, endured Saturn's shadow during deep **tapasya** (austerity).

But it was **Hanuman**, the embodiment of strength and devotion, who stood in Saturn's gaze without fear.

Not because he was more powerful, but because he was pure. Empty of ego. Anchored in duty. Free from personal desire.

That is the secret.

Saturn's trials don't break those who live in truth. They only destroy illusion.

My Saturn Years: A Personal Reckoning

From age 13 to 25, I lived under Saturn's direct influence.

First through **Sade Sati**, the seven-and-a-half-year transit that astrologers warn of.

Then through **Janma Shani**, where Saturn sits on your moon, your emotional self.

It wasn't just astrology. It was real.

Thirteen years of spiritual boot camp.

Of loss, self-doubt, broken health, faded dreams, near silence, and the recurring echo: *Why me?*

But now I know why.

Saturn was pruning me.

Peeling off every false identity, every inherited belief, every laziness, every escape route.

I used to cry in secret, not knowing that the very tears I shed were salt washing away the old self.

And now?

I'm still here.

Not healed, perhaps, but **refined**.

Jung and the Saturn Shadow

Carl Jung, the great psychoanalyst, spoke of the **Shadow**, the unconscious parts of ourselves we avoid. The parts that carry shame, anger, guilt, fear. Not because they are bad, but because they are buried.

Saturn, in astrological psychology, is the force that *demands* we face the Shadow.

It brings us experiences that reflect our unresolved wounds:

> The same kind of relationship again and again.
>
> The same failure in new forms.
>
> The same voice inside whispering, *"You're not enough."*

Until we stop blaming the outside.

Until we realize, it was never about them. It was about **us**.

This is Saturn's mirror. Unforgiving, yes. But also the most honest reflection we'll ever see.

Delay Is Not Denial, It Is Deepening

We live in a culture of urgency.

If it doesn't happen now, we think it's not meant to be.

If the love doesn't come, the job doesn't land, the healing doesn't arrive, we assume it's failure.

But Saturn teaches another language.

The language of time.

Saturn's delays are not denials. They are **maturing**.

Like soil pressed before seed breaks.

Like silence before sunrise.

The gift is real, but only when *you are real enough to receive it.*

Saturn Return: The Karmic Reckoning

Around the age of 28 to 30, everyone experiences a **Saturn Return**, when Saturn comes back to the exact position it occupied at the moment of your birth.

It is one of life's great initiations.

You may feel your world shake.

You may question everything, relationships, career, identity, belief systems.

You may lose what no longer serves you, or be asked to step into something bigger than you've ever dared before.

If you resist it, it feels like destruction.

If you embrace it, it becomes a doorway.

Your Saturn Return is the universe asking you:

> "Are you still the person others made you?

Or are you ready to become who you truly are?"

It is a sacred storm. But it clears the way for sovereignty.

Cosmic Exercise: Saturn Reflection Journal

You don't need to believe in astrology to do this.

Just believe that **life has been trying to teach you something**, and now, you're finally ready to listen.

In your journal, ask yourself:

1. What has life delayed for me, and how did that delay deepen me?
2. What experiences have repeated, what is the unseen pattern?
3. Where have I tried to escape responsibility, and what happened when I avoided it?
4. What pain still lingers… because I never gave it my honest attention?
5. What masks have I worn to avoid being vulnerable?

Write slowly. With honesty. With silence.

Let Saturn speak through your memories.

Then ask:

> "If these were not punishments, what were they preparing me for?"

And most importantly:

> "Am I willing to grow now, without needing life to break me again?"

Closing Reflection

You don't heal by avoiding Saturn. You heal by **dancing with it**.

You rise not despite the delays, the losses, the hardships, but *through them*.

Saturn does not demand perfection.

It demands truth.

And if you give it that, however messy, however slow, it will reward you not with comfort, but with **depth**.

Not with ease, but with **wisdom**.

You will stand taller.

Not because life became easier…

But because you stopped shrinking when it didn't.

That's Saturn's gift.

The one you only see when you stop running.

The one that turns karma into clarity.

The one that transforms a wounded human… into a grounded soul.

Suffering and Spiritual Alchemy

Turning Wounds Into Wisdom

"Just when the caterpillar thought the world was over, it became a butterfly."

There was a time I didn't want to be here.

Not in a dramatic, loud way.

It was quieter than that, like a silent drowning. Like walking through life wearing a smile that never touched the bones. Like carrying a weight you didn't know how to name, so you called it normal.

It's strange how the darkest thoughts don't always look like screaming or chaos. Sometimes, they show up as a perfectly made bed you don't want to leave. A phone full of contacts you never call. A life that looks fine from the outside but feels hollow on the inside.

At one point, I started believing I wasn't built for this world. Maybe something was wrong with me. That everyone else had some secret instruction manual for happiness, for belonging, for peace, and mine got lost on the way.

What I didn't know then... was that pain has intelligence.

And more importantly, pain has direction.

Viktor Frankl & The Meaning Hidden in Suffering

Years later, I came across a book that rearranged the furniture of my soul.

Man's Search for Meaning, by Viktor Frankl.

Frankl was a psychiatrist, but that wasn't what made his words sacred. What made them sacred was that they were born from the concentration camps of Auschwitz, where he lost his entire family, and nearly his own life.

He saw people die not from starvation or beatings, but from hopelessness. And what he discovered was revolutionary:

> *"Those who have a 'why' to live can bear almost any 'how.'"*

Suffering, he wrote, was not optional. But suffering without **meaning**, that was unbearable.

That line cracked something open inside me.

What if my pain wasn't here to punish me, but to **teach** me?

What if the part of me that wanted to die… was actually the part of me that desperately wanted to *live differently?*

The Fire as Teacher, Pema Chödrön and Walking Into Fear

I found another teacher in the Buddhist nun, **Pema Chödrön**, and her sacred book *The Places That Scare You*.

She didn't speak like a guru. She spoke like a fellow human who had sat with her pain long enough to let it speak.

Her wisdom was radical:

> *"The most difficult times for many of us are the ones we give ourselves."*

And yet, those are the moments where we can also find our deepest awakening, if we don't run from them.

Pain, she said, wasn't something to conquer or banish.

It was something to *enter*, like a fire that didn't burn you, but transformed you.

And I started wondering:

What if I stopped escaping my pain… and instead listened to it?

What if every anxiety, every heartbreak, every failure was actually a messenger?

What if suffering wasn't my enemy, but my greatest invitation?

When Things Fall Apart, Let Them.

When Things Fall Apart was another book I found during my unraveling. Another gentle hand in the dark.

I began to realize:

You don't *get over* suffering.

You *alchemize* it.

You take the raw, unfiltered grief and run it through the fire of your awareness. You let it shake you. Break you. Hollow you out. And then you wait, not to go back to who you were, but to *become* who you were always meant to be.

This is the ancient art of **spiritual alchemy**.

What Is Alchemy, Really?

In ancient traditions, alchemy was the mystical science of turning lead into gold.

But on the spiritual path, it means turning pain into power.

Wounds into wisdom.

Sorrow into sacredness.

It is what happens when you stop asking, *"Why did this happen to me?"*

And start asking, *"What is this here to awaken in me?"*

That shift… changes everything.

My Inner Fire

I won't pretend it's easy.

There were nights when I stared at the ceiling, asking God to take the ache away.

There were mornings when I felt like my soul had rusted overnight.

But here's what I've learned:

You don't find light **in spite of** the darkness.

You find it **inside** the darkness.

You walk through hell, and instead of letting it consume you, you learn to carry fire in your chest.

I started journaling.

I started meditating, not to escape, but to make contact with the parts of myself I had banished.

I began whispering to my pain:

> "You didn't deserve the suffering. But you deserve the peace now."

And slowly, the armor began to fall.

Not all at once.

But enough for light to enter.

You Are Not Broken, You Are Becoming

You don't need to be fixed.

You are not a mistake.

What you need is to witness your own soul. To look at the scar and say:

> "I survived that."

"I grew from that."

"And maybe, I can use that pain to help someone else."

That's when suffering becomes sacred.

That's when it becomes **medicine**, not just for you, but for the world.

Spiritual Prompt: The Alchemy Question

Take a few minutes. Light a candle if you'd like. Close your eyes.

Now ask yourself:

> **"What was life trying to teach me through the pain I once hated the most?"**

Don't rush the answer. Don't filter it.

You may cry.

You may go quiet.

That's okay.

You're not doing this to fix anything.

You're doing this to *remember* who you are beneath the wound.

Because that's where your gold is.

And that gold… is what the world desperately needs.

Ancestral Strength: The Grandmother Story

"She prayed not to be saved from the fire, but to survive it with grace."

In every family, there is one silent pillar.

Not the loudest voice.

Not the wealthiest.

Not the one with accolades.

But the one who endured the most, and still gave love.

For me, that was my grandmother.

She never gave speeches, never wrote in journals.

But her whole life was scripture.

A prayer in motion.

A Girl with a God-Sized Strength

She was married off at sixteen, which, in her village, was already considered "late."

Her husband, my grandfather, was a man from another state. An alcoholic. A stranger not just in language, but in soul.

She didn't marry a man; she married his battles.

From the very first day, she was tested.

There were no flowers. No love songs.

Only a crumbling home with hungry mouths and fists that didn't know how to love.

She bore four children into that chaos.

Raised them with bare hands, often feeding them less than she fed herself.

And through it all, the hunger, the humiliation, the pain, she kept her spine straight.

Not out of pride…

But out of **faith**.

She never asked, *"Why me?"*

She asked, *"How can I still love in this?"*

That was her power: **devotion over despair**.

Silence as Strength

She never complained.

Even when her husband beat her, even when her own mother-in-law crushed her spirit with daily insults, she never responded with bitterness.

I used to think she was weak for being quiet.

But I understand now:

It takes **tremendous strength to be silent when your dignity is bleeding**.

Her silence wasn't submission.

It was sacred.

Like the earth, absorbing every storm, yet still blooming the next season.

Prayers Not for Rescue, but Resilience

What broke me most was how she prayed.

Not as a woman begging for a miracle, but as a soul whispering to the Divine like He was her old friend.

Each morning, before dawn, she would wake up, light a diya, and fold her hands in front of a tiny altar.

And with tears in her eyes, she would say:

> "Thank you for another day. Give me the strength to do what is right."

She never asked God to change her fate.

She only asked for the grace to carry it.

That's the kind of woman she was.

A woman who walked through fire without turning to ash.

A woman whose devotion didn't come from comfort, but from choosing **dignity in surrender**.

The Divine Feminine, Embodied

In mythology, we worship Durga, Kali, Lakshmi, goddesses who slay demons, create worlds, sustain life.

But my grandmother was all of them, wrapped in a cotton saree, feet cracked from work, eyes soft with stories she never told.

She didn't need temples to be divine.

She **was** the temple.

And the older I get, the more I realize… her resilience runs in my blood.

Her silence taught me more about power than any motivational speech.

Her pain taught me more about love than any romantic poem.

Her endurance?

It's my inheritance.

Legacy Lives in Love

The world may never know her name.

There will be no books about her.

No documentaries.

But I am her legacy.

And I'm writing these words so she's remembered not just as someone who survived…

But as someone who **transformed suffering into sacredness**.

She loved, even when she wasn't loved back.

She gave, even when she was empty.

She prayed, even when life felt godless.

And somehow, she passed that quiet power to me.

So now, when life feels unfair, I close my eyes and ask:

> *What would she do?*

And I hear her spirit whisper:

> *"Stand tall. Bow only to the Divine. Choose love."*

Legacy Practice: Write a Letter of Gratitude to an Ancestor

We all come from a line of survivors.

People who lived through wars, heartbreaks, poverty, injustice, illness… and still, somehow, kept love alive.

Take a moment.

Sit in silence.

Light a candle if you wish.

Then write a letter to one of them, even if you never met them.

Maybe it's your grandmother.

Maybe a great-uncle.

Maybe even a cultural ancestor who walked a path you now benefit from.

In the letter, thank them.

For their sacrifices.

For their strength.

For carrying forward a life you now live.

Here's how it can begin:

> "Dear One,
>
> I may not know your full story, but I feel you in mine.
>
> Your strength flows in my veins.
>
> Your love made this life possible.
>
> Thank you for walking when the path was hard…
>
> So I could run when it became clear."

Let the letter flow.

Let your spirit connect.

Because healing isn't just individual, it's ancestral.

And when you thank those who came before you…

You remember who you are.

You are not just one person.

You are a living echo of every soul who refused to give up.

That's what my grandmother taught me.

And now, I hope... she teaches you too.

Rage, God, and Returning to Faith

I didn't just lose faith.

I *burned it.*

I called it foolish. I mocked it. I blamed it for everything I couldn't control.

When life hurt, really hurt, I didn't kneel down. I clenched my fists.

I argued with my grandmother, the most faithful woman I knew.

She used to pray before dawn, folding her hands in front of the flame. I used to watch her lips move silently, her eyes moist with belief.

And I remember once, in my lowest moment, shouting:

> "Why do you keep praying? Where was your God when you were suffering?"

Her answer still echoes inside me:

"He was with me… that's why I survived."

I didn't understand it then. I didn't want to. I was too angry.

A God I Couldn't Trust

If God was real, why did He give me this life?

Why the pain? The shame? The loneliness that turned into panic attacks at night?

And so, I turned my back on Him.

I thought that made me strong.

But truthfully?

It just made me alone.

Spiritual atheism is a cold silence.

It doesn't offer comfort in the night.

It doesn't hold you when you're breaking.

It only says: "You're on your own."

And for a long time… I believed I was.

Holy Rage

No one talks about the *rage* that can exist between a soul and its Creator.

But it's there, in sacred texts, in our myths, in the quiet tears of those who feel abandoned by something they once trusted.

Job in the Bible lost everything, children, wealth, health.

And he screamed to God: "Why me?"

Sita was exiled to the forest even after proving her purity.

Jesus cried out on the cross:

> "My God, my God, why have you forsaken me?"

Even the most divine have felt *divinely deserted.*

Faith Isn't What We Think It Is

I used to think faith meant believing God exists.

But now I know:

Faith is trusting, even when you don't.

It's showing up to the silence.

It's lighting a diya with tears in your eyes and no idea if anyone's listening.

It's choosing to love a God who feels distant... because somewhere in your bones, you *remember* He's never truly gone.

The most tested are often the most chosen.

Not because they are special.

But because their soul came here to *remember* through resistance.

My Grandmother's Faith: A Mirror

After one especially bitter argument, my grandmother just smiled.

She didn't defend God. She didn't argue. She simply said:

> "One day, when you're ready, He will meet you again. Even your anger is a prayer."

That stayed with me.

Because I realized, even when I was raging, I wasn't disconnected.

Anger still speaks to God.

Silence still reaches Him.

Pain still touches heaven.

And slowly, my walls began to crumble.

Not in a dramatic moment.

But gently.

One silent sit in the early morning light.

One whisper of, "If You're real… I need You."

No lightning. No visions.

Just… peace.

The first peace I'd felt in years.

Rebuilding, Not Replacing

I didn't return to religion.

I returned to *relationship*.

It wasn't about rituals anymore.

It was about raw truth.

I sat in silence and said things I'd never dared say:

> "I'm angry with You."
>
> "I feel abandoned."
>
> "Why did You let that happen?"
>
> "Where were You when I cried myself to sleep?"
>
> "I don't know if I can believe again."

And somewhere in that honesty… I began to feel held.

Not judged. Not punished.

Held.

Because that's what real faith is, not a performance, but a presence.

Soul Practice: Raw Prayer

Don't recite. Don't chant.

Just speak.

To God, to the Universe, to your Higher Self, however you name the sacred.

No filter.

No pretending.

Sit in silence.

And speak your truth.

Say:

- "I'm tired."
- "I'm scared."
- "I don't know who I am anymore."
- "Why did You let them hurt me?"
- "Where were You when I needed You?"

Say it all.

Because *even anger is a form of connection.*

Even rage is a form of reaching.

You're not blaspheming.

You're being real.

And that's what the Divine longs for,

Not your perfection.

Not your obedience.

Your truth.

One day, you will look back and see:

Even in your darkest moments, something was holding you.

And maybe that something was God.

Maybe it was your soul.

Maybe it was your grandmother's prayers.

Maybe it was all the same thing.

Faith doesn't mean you never doubt.

It means you keep walking anyway.

Because some part of you knows:

> **Love never left.**
>
> You just needed time… to come home.

The Path of Surrender

I used to think I wanted to become an Aghori at some point.

To leave everything behind.

To live at the edge of the world, near death, ash-smeared, fearless, untouched by desire, unbothered by society.

It felt like the highest form of spirituality.

What could be more powerful than walking through cremation grounds with no fear of anything?

But as I grew, or perhaps, as I shattered, something deeper whispered inside me:

> "The greatest renunciation is not found in fire or ash.
>
> It's in softening your heart in a world that keeps hardening it."

The Illusion of Power

I once believed surrender meant giving up.

Losing. Failing. Folding your hands when you should be fighting.

But life taught me otherwise.

It showed me that the strongest people are not those who control everything, but those who trust when nothing is in their control.

I saw that real power isn't loud. It's not about dominating others or detaching from everything.

Sometimes, power is letting yourself cry.

Sometimes, it's letting someone love you, even when you feel unlovable.

Sometimes, it's whispering to the sky:

> "I can't carry this anymore. I surrender it to You."

What the Aghoris Know

The Aghori path is not what most people imagine.

Yes, they live by burning ghats. Yes, they meditate on death.

But their purpose isn't horror, it's transcendence.

They go beyond illusion, beyond fear, shame, body, mind, ego.

They see God in everything:

in bones, in blood, in the silence of the graveyard.

Because *if God is not in death, then He is not in life either.*

But I've come to realize: you don't need to live like an Aghori to walk their truth.

You can live in the heart of a family.

You can raise children. Pay bills. Sit in traffic. Heal from heartbreak.

And still walk the fire of surrender, every single day.

The Highest Renunciation

I used to fantasize about running away.

Renouncing society. Becoming nobody. Escaping this complicated life.

But the real renunciation… is right here.

> It is choosing forgiveness when revenge feels easier.

It is choosing compassion in the face of cruelty.

It is choosing to *stay*, in love, in faith, in service, when your ego screams "leave."

It is washing dishes, caring for your parents, showing up for work, staying silent when your pride wants to win.

Renunciation isn't outer. It's inner.

It's letting go of the stories you cling to.

The pain you nurse.

The image you protect.

The illusion that *you* are in control.

Surrender doesn't say, "I give up."

It says, "I give it up, to something greater than me."

From Control to Trust

We all want control.

We want timelines, guarantees, answers that fit inside spreadsheets and vision boards.

But life doesn't operate on demand.

It teaches through mystery. Through waiting. Through uncertainty. Through broken plans that lead to better paths.

And somewhere along the way, you learn:

> Control is a burden.

> Trust is a freedom.

You stop gripping the wheel and begin to feel the wind.

You stop forcing your way through the storm and begin to dance in the rain.

You stop asking, "Why me?" and start asking, "What is life inviting me to become?"

The Soft Warrior

In this world, hardness is rewarded.

Sharp minds. Strong opinions. Unbreakable facades.

But I've come to admire a different kind of warrior.

The one who softens.

Who doesn't build higher walls, but deeper roots.

Who doesn't need to win every battle, because they've already made peace within.

Who loves in a way that feels like prayer.

Who walks through chaos without needing to control it.

This kind of warrior walks the path of surrender.

Not because they are weak.

But because they know:

Grace works better than force.

Stillness works deeper than struggle.

Daily Mantra Practice: Let Go. Let God. Let Grace.

Here's a practice I whisper to myself every morning. Maybe you'll want to try it too.

Step 1: Sit quietly. Breathe. Place your hand over your heart.

Feel your breath. Feel your weight. Feel the moment.

Step 2: On each inhale, silently say: "Let Go."

Let go of what didn't happen. Let go of yesterday. Let go of the story.

Step 3: On the next exhale, whisper: "Let God."

Let life take over. Let something wiser than your mind hold the steering wheel.

Step 4: On the next breath, say: "Let Grace."

Allow yourself to receive what's already trying to find you.

Repeat as needed.

Not as a chant. Not as a performance.

As a return, to peace. To humility. To truth.

Sometimes, I still wish I could walk the riverbanks of Kashi, away from it all.

But life has whispered to me:

> "You are already at the sacred ghat. It is your life."

> "The burning ground is not outside. It is inside your chest, where your ego burns to ash, and your soul rises clean."

I thought I wanted to become an Aghori.

But maybe... I already am one.

Not through ashes on my skin,

but through surrender in my soul.

Practical Healing Practices

We all long to heal. But longing isn't enough.

At some point, the soul whispers, "You've felt enough. Now it's time to *do*."

Healing is not a mystical peak to reach; it's a daily walk. A discipline of softness. An art of returning.

The deeper I walked into my own pain, the more I realized: we don't need a miracle. We need practices.

Simple, soulful rituals that help the heart breathe again. That pull our identity back from old pain, and place it in the hands of possibility.

Here are a few of the most potent tools that have transformed my journey, each one an act of self-respect.

Letter to Your Younger Self

This is where it begins: with the child within.

Sit down. Light a candle if you wish. Close your eyes and think of a version of you who once felt forgotten, shamed, or left behind. Maybe it was you at five years old, confused by a world that didn't make sense. Maybe you at fifteen, carrying pain that no one saw.

Now write to them.

Not as a stranger. As the adult you needed back then.

Say the words you were dying to hear:

"You did your best."

"I'm so proud of you."

"It wasn't your fault."

"You didn't deserve what happened, but you deserve healing now."

Let the tears come. Let the pen speak. You're not just writing, you're reclaiming.

Daily Emotional Check-In

Most of us move through life like a closed room, unaware of what's happening inside.

Healing starts with presence.

Every morning or evening, pause. Place a hand over your chest and ask:

- What am I feeling right now?
- Where do I feel it in my body?
- What might this emotion be trying to teach me?

There is no right or wrong answer. There is only honesty. And honesty is where healing breathes.

The Ho'oponopono Prayer

A Hawaiian Ritual of Reconciliation & Forgiveness

Simple. Gentle. Powerful.

Repeat these four lines slowly, to yourself, to someone you're hurt by, or to the universe:

> I'm sorry.
>
> Please forgive me.
>
> Thank you.
>
> I love you.

These words carry centuries of spiritual wisdom. They remind us that even pain we didn't cause can still be healed by the love we choose.

Say them. Whisper them. Let them wash over your guilt, shame, and grief.

Not to erase your past, but to cleanse your soul from carrying it further.

Saturn Shadow Mapping

Saturn, the great cosmic teacher, doesn't only test us through suffering. He also invites us to see the parts of ourselves we avoid.

Create a Saturn Map:

- **Write down the top three areas where life keeps testing you** (delays, relationships, self-worth, etc.)

- **Note your emotional reactions** (anger, control, avoidance)

- **Now ask: What fear or shadow might be underneath this?**

Is it fear of failure? Fear of being seen? Old guilt?

Now, in the same journal, write: *What has Saturn taught me through this?*

Turn karmic pain into conscious power.

Journal Prompts to Return to Wholeness

Take a quiet moment, maybe with tea or soft music, and explore these:

- **"What am I ready to forgive in myself?"**

- Most of us hold grudges against our past self. It's time to release.

- **"What pain am I still using as identity?"**

- Are you still defining yourself by old wounds? It's okay. But now, is it still true?

- **"What would healing look like, if I believed I deserved it?"**

- This one may break you open. And that's good. Because what comes after the breaking... is light.

These are not just tools. They are sacred rituals. Not to fix you, but to return you. To wholeness. To softness. To a soul no longer led by wounds, but by wisdom.

Begin with one. Let it lead you. Healing isn't loud. It's a quiet morning. A whisper in the dark. A hand reaching back in time to say: *"I see you. I love you. We made it."*

Final Blessing: You Are the Light Beyond the Wound

You were never broken.

Only buried.

Not beneath rubble, not beneath failure, but beneath layers, of silence, of fear, of the years when no one truly saw you. Beneath the moments where you were too brave to cry. Beneath the smiles you wore like armor. Beneath the pain you called "normal" just to survive.

But within all of that…

There was always a flame.

Tiny, flickering, hidden, yet eternal. The flame of your *Higher Self*. Watching. Waiting. Loving you anyway.

The version of you that remembers.

The part of you that never believed the lies, not the ones the world told you, and not the ones you told yourself to make the world more bearable.

Because you, dear soul, were never too much.

Never too late.

Never too broken to bloom.

You were just… buried. And now, you are remembering.

You are rising.

This chapter of your life is not the end. It's the turning. The quiet revolution where you choose, not to erase the past, but to embrace it as your sacred soil.

Your pain was not a punishment.

It was a passage.

Your delays were not denials.

They were divine detours.

And now, as you close this chapter, I ask you not to rush. Don't run from the tears if they come. Let them fall. They are holy. They are honest. They are your body's way of releasing lifetimes of unspoken prayers.

If your heart is aching, it means it's still alive.

If your breath is shaky, it means you're still willing.

And if you feel even a flicker of hope,

then *you're already healing.*

Because healing is not perfection.

It's not walking without scars.

It's walking with grace, with tenderness, through the same places that once shattered you… and saying:

"I am still here."

"I still believe."

"I am choosing love over fear, again and again and again."

So yes, feel. Deeply.

Because feeling is how the soul breathes.

Yes, heal.

Because you deserve the peace that was once denied to you.

Yes, rise.

Not as someone who never fell,

but as someone who *fell and still rose.*

Let this not be your end.

Let this be your becoming.

Let this be the moment you look back on one day and whisper:

"That was the moment I returned to myself."

Blessing for the Reader

May your wounds become windows.

May your shadows become teachers.

May your pain become purpose.

And may your heart, no matter how many storms it has weathered,

remain soft.

And sacred.

And shining.

Because you, exactly as you are, not when you're "better," not when you're "fixed", are the miracle.

You are the light beyond the wound.

You are the soul rising from the story.

And the world is lucky to have you still in it.

Still breathing.

Still believing.

Keep going.

You're closer than you think.

8

Aligning Energy, Aura, And Values

There comes a moment, after the storms, after the breakdowns, after the silence, when you begin to sense something deeper than words. A vibration. A pull. A quiet knowing. That's your inner compass.

You start realizing that life isn't just about what you do, it's about how you feel when you do it. It's not just about chasing goals. It's about aligning your energy, values, and purpose into one powerful current. Because without that alignment, you're just moving, not evolving.

Understanding Energy & Aura

What Is Energy? And Why Does It Matter?

Everything is energy. You, me, this page, the thoughts in your mind, the space in this room. You've felt it before, that sudden heaviness around someone who's angry, that lightness when you walk into nature, or that gut feeling that something's not right. That's energy. And you can read it. In fact, you already are, all the time.

In spirituality, your aura reflects your energy field, a subtle force that surrounds your body and communicates your inner state to the world. When your energy is scattered, heavy, or blocked, everything feels off, your relationships, your decisions, even your health. But when your energy is aligned with your core truth, life begins to flow.

You meet the right people. You get the right ideas. You move with a quiet confidence.

Aligning Your Values, Passions & Purpose

- **Values** = What you stand for. Your soul's ethics.
- **Passions** = What lights you up. What gives you energy.
- **Purpose** = The deeper why behind your actions. The service you bring to the world.

When these three align, you feel it in your body. You're not faking it. You're not drained. You're not lost. You become a tuning fork, resonating with the right people, places, and opportunities.

How to Read Your Own Energy

- Check how your body feels after doing something.
- Observe your emotions around certain people.
- Listen to the silence within.

Your body always knows. It's your compass.

Advanced Aura Reading & Elemental Mastery

There comes a point in your spiritual journey when intuition becomes precision.

Where "vibes" aren't just felt vaguely, they're traced, identified, and worked with like sacred tools.

This is not beginner's energy work. This is inner alchemy.

This is what the masters knew.

Vibrational Listening

In ancient Himalayan caves, yogis didn't "see" auras in colors.

They **listened**.

To silence.

To sensation.

To the soft murmur of presence itself.

This is called **vibrational listening**, the practice of sensing energy not just with the eyes, but with the entire nervous system.

▶ How to Practice Vibrational Listening

- **Step 1: Enter Prolonged Silence**
- Sit in complete silence (ideally early morning or twilight). No phone. No music. No agenda. Just *presence*.

- **Step 2: Body Scanning Without Thought**

- Bring your attention from the crown of your head to your toes, pausing wherever you feel "heat," "coolness," "density," or "pull." These are aura pockets, storing information.

- **Step 3: Observe Energy Shifts Around Others**

- In conversations, don't just listen to words. Feel your body, does your solar plexus tighten? Do you feel a pressure behind your eyes? That's energy information.

Over time, you'll begin to know things without being told.

You'll sense moods before people speak.

You'll even read environments by "listening" to the energetic silence between objects.

> "The quieter you become, the more you hear." – Ram Dass

Elemental Aura Cleansing

The Vedas taught that the body is made of **Pancha Mahabhuta**, the Five Great Elements:

Earth (Prithvi), Water (Apas/Soma), Fire (Agni/Surya), Air (Vayu), and **Space (Akasha).**

Your aura, your electromagnetic energy field, holds imprints from each.

When out of balance, these elements can trap emotional, mental, or karmic debris in the field.

The goal of **Elemental Mastery** is to harmonize your aura through nature's forces, not just symbolically, but vibrationally.

1. Earth (Prithvi) – Stabilize and Ground

Symptoms of Earth Deficiency in Aura:

- Anxiety, spaciness, overthinking
- Disconnection from the body or reality

Healing Practices:

- Walk barefoot on natural ground (earthing).
- Sit under large trees and lean your spine against them, trees discharge energetic noise.
- Sleep on cotton or linen, avoid synthetics, which disrupt electromagnetic absorption.
- Place raw crystals like **black tourmaline** or **hematite** at the base of your feet while meditating.

"Earth doesn't judge your chaos, she absorbs it."

2. Water (Soma) – Release and Flow

Symptoms of Water Blockage:

- Emotional numbness or overwhelm

- Holding onto grief, guilt, or shame

Healing Practices:

- Soak in warm **salt water baths** (Himalayan or sea salt) to dissolve emotional charge.

- Visualize pain or memory dissolving into the water and draining away.

- Practice *Jala Neti* (water nasal cleansing) to clear pranic channels.

- Drink water mindfully. Bless it. Water holds memory, you can program it.

Advanced: Whisper forgiveness into a glass of water. Drink it. Let the words become your aura.

3. Air (Vayu) – Clarity and Movement

Symptoms of Air Disturbance:

- Racing thoughts, indecision

- Energy "stuck" in the head or throat

Healing Practices:

- **Pranayama (breathwork)**, especially Nadi Shodhana (alternate nostril breathing) and Bhramari (humming bee breath).

- Burn sacred smoke: **Dhoop, camphor, Palo Santo**, or **sage**.

- Open windows often, stagnant air creates stagnant aura.

- Whisper affirmations into the air around you: "My mind is still. My breath is divine."

Advanced: Practice **inner wind circulation** (used in Tibetan Vajrayana), where breath is directed into chakras to break subtle blocks.

4. Fire (Surya/Agni) – Purify and Activate

Symptoms of Fire Imbalance:

- Burnout or lethargy
- Resentment, unprocessed anger

Healing Practices:

- **Trataka (flame gazing)**, stare at a candle flame without blinking for 2–5 minutes. Close your eyes and visualize it at the heart.

- Recite **Surya mantras** (e.g., *Om Suryaya Namaha*) at sunrise.

- Perform Agnihotra or simple fire offerings with intention (write what you release, burn it).

- Sunbathing (10–20 minutes) to activate solar plexus and aura expansion.

Advanced: Initiate **inner fire meditation** (*Tummo*), used by Tibetan monks to awaken the sacred flame at the navel (Manipura chakra), igniting spiritual energy.

Space (Akasha) – Expand and Transcend

Though often forgotten, **Akasha** is the most subtle and powerful element. It's the ether, the divine field of **pure potential**.

Symptoms of Space Disharmony:

- Feeling lost, spiritually disconnected
- Lack of inspiration or creative flow

Healing Practices:

- Sit in **pure stillness** (no goals, no thoughts).
- Practice **OM chanting** to awaken the Akashic vibration.
- Journal into silence, don't write with logic, let words arrive from the void.
- Speak less. Listen more. Space is fed by silence.

Advanced: Tap into the **Akashic Field**, where all soul memory is stored, through deep trance meditations, or intuitive automatic writing.

Initiation: Becoming an Elemental Alchemist

You are not just healing your aura.

You are becoming its **master sculptor**.

You are aligning your field with the forces of creation, Earth, Water, Air, Fire, and Space, as they exist both **within you** and **around you**.

This is the level of mastery where aura work stops being spiritual hygiene and becomes **spiritual architecture**.

You don't just protect your energy.

You build it into a **temple**.

And each element is your brick.

Each ritual is your sacred flame.

Each silence is a chisel carving out your higher self.

Soul Practice: The 5-Element Aura Reset

Once a week (preferably on Sundays or Full Moons), perform a **5-step aura cleansing ritual**, using one practice from each element.

Write your observations after each:

- How did your breath change?
- Did emotions rise or soften?
- Did intuition sharpen or become silent?

Track these over time.

This is your **energy fingerprint** evolving.

Protection – Your Energetic Shield

There's a reason spiritual masters across traditions begin the day not with to-do lists, but with **alignment** and **protection**.

They know that in a world full of noise, agendas, and unconscious projections, your greatest asset is not just your wisdom,

It's your **energy sovereignty**.

Because energy doesn't lie.

It absorbs.

It reflects.

It remembers.

And unless you consciously **protect your field**, you will carry what is not yours:

Other people's doubts.

Collective fear.

Unspoken tension.

Even karmic dust that isn't yours to clean.

Let's learn how to **shield** your aura, not out of fear, but from sacred self-respect.

1. Breath + Light Visualization

This is a foundational practice used by mystics, monks, and Reiki masters across cultures.

How to Practice:

- Sit or stand with your spine upright.

- Inhale deeply through your nose and visualize **pure white light** entering your crown (top of your head).

- As you **exhale**, visualize grey or dusty smoke leaving your body, the remnants of external energy or emotional weight.

- Now, on the next few breaths, **build a sphere of light** around your body, soft, radiant, yet impenetrable.

- Say aloud or internally:

    "Only truth, light, and peace may enter my space.

    What is not mine, I now release."

This is not just imagination.

Your **nervous system**, **mind**, and **aura** are all being attuned by your intention.

Over time, you will literally *feel* the difference before and after this daily practice.

2. Grounding Through Body Awareness

When energy is scattered, you're more easily influenced.

But when you're grounded, your presence becomes impenetrable.

Practice:

- Sit still. Feel your feet firmly touching the ground.
- Place one hand on your **chest** and the other on your **belly**.
- Take slow breaths and feel your body as *home*, not just a vessel.
- With every exhale, silently repeat:
- "I am here. I am safe. I am sovereign."

This is how the earth reminds you:

You belong here.

And no one else decides what lives in your field.

3. Decluttering Emotional Ties

Often, what leaks our energy is not loud, it's lingering.

- That friend you haven't spoken to, but still think about.
- That ex you said you moved on from, but still feel in your chest.
- That boss or parent or stranger whose words left an imprint.

These are **energetic cords**, invisible threads that bind you to others, often unconsciously.

Cord-Cutting Mantra:

Sit quietly. Bring the person or situation to mind.

Place your hand on your heart.

Say:

> "I lovingly release all energy that does not belong to me.
>
> I return it to its source with peace."

You don't need to hate or fight it.

Release **with grace**.

That's how masters stay light.

4. Affirmations for Energetic Boundaries

Words program your field like sacred code.

They act like **energetic passwords**, telling your subconscious what to allow and what to block.

Use these:

- "My energy is mine. It is sacred and protected."
- "What is not mine cannot stay. What is mine cannot be taken."
- "I attract truth. I release distortion."
- "I do not absorb projections. I reflect clarity."

Say them daily, in front of a mirror, during breathwork, or in silence.

Speak not as a victim, but as a **guardian of your temple**.

Reiki: The Art of Energy Healing

One of the most profound tools for energetic protection, cleansing, and realignment is **Reiki**, a Japanese healing technique that channels **universal life force energy** (also called *ki*, *prana*, or *chi*) through the hands.

The word **Reiki** comes from:

- **Rei** = "Universal"

- **Ki** = "Life energy"

What Reiki Does:

- Clears blockages in your **chakras** and **meridians**

- Restores emotional balance

- Strengthens your **aura**

- Protects you from energy leakage

- Allows healing energy to **flow through**, not just to, you

How It Works:

A certified **Reiki practitioner** (or yourself, once attuned) places hands lightly on or above specific areas of your body (chakras).

There is **no force**.

Just presence.

Just intention.

As the Reiki flows, it knows exactly what to do, like a river remembering its path.

Your body, mind, and spirit reorganize themselves around this higher frequency.

> Reiki isn't about "doing."

> It's about **becoming a channel** for pure healing consciousness.

▶ How to Begin Reiki Practices at Home:

(Even without formal training, you can begin the intention-based practice)

1. Sit in silence. Rub your hands together briskly to awaken your palms (your healing centers).

2. Close your eyes and place your hands over your **heart**, **head**, or **navel**.

3. Breathe deeply and say:

4. "Let life force flow through me. Let all that blocks be dissolved in light."

5. Stay here for 5–10 minutes, simply **feeling**.

6. Afterward, drink water. Journal if needed.

If you're called, consider learning from a **certified Reiki Master**, the path is gentle, yet immensely powerful.

Once attuned, you can perform Reiki on yourself daily to fortify your aura.

Final Thought: Your Field is Your Fortress

Protection is not about hiding.

It's about remembering what you're made of, **pure light**, **conscious breath**, **earth wisdom**, and **cosmic grace**.

When your field is clear and strong:

- People feel it without you speaking.
- Negativity dissolves before reaching you.
- Peace becomes your default setting.

    "The most powerful form of protection is presence.

    When you are fully in your body, in your breath, in your truth, nothing can override you."

Guard your energy with love.

Not as a defense,

But as a devotion to your most sacred self.

Daily Aura Cleansing Techniques

"You cleanse your body daily, why not your soul?"

Your aura is your **first skin**.

Invisible, but felt.

Soft, yet strong.

It absorbs what you experience and quietly stores the emotions, words, and energies you didn't have time to process.

And over time, like unwashed windows, the light within becomes blurred.

That's why daily **energetic hygiene** is not a luxury.

It's spiritual survival.

Let these sacred techniques become your daily rituals, not as chores, but as conversations with your soul.

1. Salt Showers or Baths

One of the oldest and most effective aura cleansing tools is salt. Ancient cultures used it to absorb spiritual residue and dissolve energetic heaviness.

How to Practice:

- Add a handful of **rock salt or sea salt** to your bath water.

- Or post-shower, rub saltwater gently over your body and rinse off.

- As the water flows, visualize every bit of stress, negativity, and emotional heaviness being washed away.

Whisper this mantra:

"I release what no longer serves.

I return to my purest light."

It's not just water.

It's a ritual of remembering.

2. Smoke Cleansing (Dhoop, Agarbatti, Camphor)

Our ancestors instinctively knew what we're just beginning to remember, **smoke carries intention**.

Fire transforms.

Smoke clears what the eyes cannot see.

How to Practice:

- Light agarbatti, dhoop, or camphor.

- Move slowly around your room, your bed, and finally, around your own body.

- Let the smoke envelop your aura, especially around the head, chest, and back.

Speak softly:

> "Let this space be clear. Let this body be sacred.
>
> I invite only love, peace, and truth."

Your energy responds not to force, but to reverence.

3. Emotional Journaling

Aura cleansing isn't always external.

Some of the deepest blockages come from **unfelt emotions**.

Prompt:

> "What am I still holding that no longer belongs to me?"

Write without judgment.

Let the ink carry what the heart couldn't say.

Grief, shame, fear, even anger, let it pour.

Then close the journal, place your hand on your heart, and say:

> "I give myself permission to let go."

This is therapy for your soul.

And your aura will shine clearer with every honest page.

4. Sound Medicine

Sound doesn't just soothe, it **shakes loose what is stuck**.

That's why monks chant.

Why temples echo with mantras.

Why ancient healers use bells, bowls, and tones.

How to Practice:

- Use **Tibetan singing bowls, OM chanting**, or sacred mantras like:
- "Ra Ma Da Sa, Sa Say So Hung"
- (A mantra for deep healing and spiritual purification.)
- Let the sound fill the room. Close your eyes and **feel** it pass through your chest, head, and spine.

Even five minutes of deep sound will **realign your aura's frequency**, from chaos to calm.

5. Breathwork & Tears (4-4-6 Practice)

You don't always need tools.

Sometimes, your own breath and tears are the most powerful medicine.

Breath Practice (4-4-6):

- Inhale for 4 seconds
- Hold for 4 seconds
- Exhale for 6 seconds (through the mouth, as if fogging a mirror)

Do this for 3–5 minutes.

Let your **exhales be your release valve**, a soft goodbye to what no longer belongs.

And if tears come, don't stop them.

Tears are your aura's **emotional rain**, washing away what words could never reach.

Final Word:

Cleansing is not about becoming perfect.

It's about **becoming present again**.

Each of these practices brings you back to your center.

They remind you that you are not here to carry the world,

You are here to **light it up** with your clearest, cleanest self.

> "Let your aura breathe.
>
> Let your energy speak before your words do."

Expanding the Aura – Your Radiance Engine

> *"You don't become magnetic by chasing. You become magnetic by radiating."*

There comes a time on the spiritual path when protection is no longer enough.

You've shielded. You've cleansed. You've let go.

Now, you're ready to **shine**.

Expanding your aura isn't about becoming more than you are, it's about becoming **fully** who you are.

It's about embodying your truth so deeply, so unapologetically, that your very presence becomes healing.

Your aura is not just a boundary, it's a **broadcast**.

And when it's strong, clean, and expansive, the world feels it before you even say a word.

What Expanding Your Aura Means

To expand your aura is to **step into your full energetic stature**,

Not with ego, but with **essence**.

It's the shift from:

- Hiding to expressing
- Withholding to flowing
- Surviving to **transmitting**

An expanded aura is your inner flame **turned outward**,

Not to burn, but to warm.

When your aura expands:

- You stop dimming your voice for comfort.

- You stop shrinking your dreams for safety.

- You **step into your field of influence**, and the right people, ideas, and synchronicities start arriving.

Because your aura is now a **yes** to life.

Signs of Aura Expansion

How do you know it's happening?

You'll feel it in your body and see it reflected in the world:

- People feel safe and soothed in your presence, even if you don't say much.

- Animals, children, strangers, they gravitate toward your calm.

- You feel centered without needing control.

- Life flows more effortlessly. What once felt blocked begins to unlock.

- You become a quiet lighthouse, not loud, but impossible to ignore.

Expansion doesn't make you better than others, it makes you more **available** to your own light.

Practices for Aura Expansion

Let these practices guide you into your luminous self, the version of you that no longer hides.

1. Embodiment: Live Fully in Your Body

Your aura strengthens when your awareness anchors into the **now,**

Not in the past. Not chasing the future. But **here.**

Walk like your steps matter.

Speak with breath behind your words.

Breathe with depth, not speed.

Try this:

- Feel the texture of your clothes.
- Listen to the sound of your footsteps.
- Notice the sensation in your palms as you move them.

The more present you are in your body, the more your aura **grounds and expands.**

> "Presence is magnetic. The body is the temple. Embodiment is the prayer."

2. Truth-Telling: Speak Without Masks

Truth is one of the most **high-frequency energies** on Earth.

When you speak your truth, your aura **vibrates with clarity**.

Not just truth in words, but in choices, boundaries, and presence.

Start here:

- Say "no" when your body tightens.
- Say "yes" when your heart opens.
- Stop pretending to be okay when you're not.

Each truth you embody clears static and widens your energetic field.

> "Truth clears what fear clouds. Say it. Live it. Let it set your energy free."

3. Intentional Movement: Dance, Flow, Breathe

Your aura thrives on **flow**, not rigidity.

Stagnant body = stagnant aura.

Move in ways that feel natural:

- Dance like no one's watching (because your soul is).
- Practice slow yoga or qigong.
- Do breath-led stretches in the morning sunlight.

Let movement be a **devotional offering**, not a performance.

As you move, feel your aura expanding outward, swirling, glowing, alive.

> "When the body moves with grace, the energy follows."

4. Soul Nourishment: What You Take In Becomes You

What you **consume**, you radiate.

Curate your energetic diet:

- Listen to music that stirs your spirit.
- Watch art that reflects your truth.
- Spend time in silence, in nature, in beauty.
- Read words that awaken, not distract.

Avoid energy that depletes, gossip, negativity, mindless noise.

Feed your senses what you want your **aura to echo**.

> "You become what you consume. Let every input feed your light."

5. Heart Radiance Visualization (5–10 min)

A simple, powerful daily ritual to consciously expand your aura.

How to Practice:

- Sit still. Close your eyes. Breathe deeply.
- Bring your awareness to the center of your chest, your **heart chakra**.

- Visualize a soft, golden light glowing in this center.

- With each inhale, feel it growing brighter.

- With each exhale, feel it expanding outward, into your arms, legs, body… beyond your skin… into the room… 3 feet… 6 feet… 10 feet around you.

Let your heart radiate like a sun.

Affirm silently:

"My energy is radiant. My presence heals.

I expand with love, not fear.

I shine, not to be seen, but to see more clearly."

You are not taking up space,

You are **offering space** for healing, truth, and soul to arrive.

Why Expansion Matters

A strong aura protects.

A **cleansed aura flows**.

But an **expanded aura** transforms.

You're no longer hiding your light.

You're using it, as a tool of love, as a compass of truth, as a **mirror for others**.

Your aura becomes a lighthouse. Not because you're shouting, but because you're **being**.

> "Don't just protect your energy. Project it.
>
> Not with noise, but with presence."

You were never meant to shrink to fit.

You were meant to **expand to serve**.

Let your energy walk into rooms before you do.

Let your radiance make introductions before your name is spoken.

Because in your highest vibration,

You don't chase.

You **attract.**

You don't prove.

You **exist fully.**

You don't seek permission.

You **become the permission.**

Becoming Magnetic

The final unfolding of your energetic truth.

> "You don't become magnetic by doing more.
>
> You become magnetic by being **real**."

There is a sacred moment on every soul's journey,

After the cleansing, the grounding, the awakening,

When you no longer strive to be *someone else*.

You remember who you already are.

Not in theory. In vibration.

Your aura, no longer burdened by old pain, no longer leaking into places that do not honor you, begins to **glow**.

Not because you are performing… but because you are finally **present**.

Your Aura Is a Beacon

You were told it was just your "vibe."

But it is far more than that.

It's your **signature**. Your **song** without words.

Your **essence** distilled into frequency.

When you enter a room with an aligned aura:

- People **pause**, not because you are loud, but because your silence carries weight.
- Eyes turn, not in judgment, but in recognition.
- You **don't chase opportunities**. You simply become the frequency that matches them.

This is not mysticism. This is **magnetism**.

> "When your aura is in alignment, life stops testing you,
>
> and begins **reflecting you**."

The Shift from Force to Flow

Magnetism is not a technique.

It is a **remembrance**.

A return to essence. A return to center.

You no longer manipulate your way through life.

You **align**.

You no longer hustle for validation.

You become the validation your younger self was waiting for.

You stop saying "yes" to what dims your light,

And suddenly, the world becomes clearer.

Cleaner. Calmer.

It's not because the world changed.

It's because **you did**.

You made a quiet choice:

To stop abandoning your energy.

To stop betraying your boundaries.

To stop outsourcing your radiance.

And that choice changed everything.

You Become the Invitation

As your aura expands, you become an **invitation** for others to remember themselves.

You don't preach healing, you embody it.

You don't demand respect, you **reflect** it.

Your grounded energy gives others permission to land in their own truth.

Your presence whispers:

> "It's safe to be whole here."

That's how the most powerful leaders are born,

Not from noise, but from **deep resonance**.

You become a mirror that does not distort.

A presence that does not compete.

A soul that does not apologize for its glow.

Radiance Without Noise

In a world obsessed with external achievement, you become a quiet rebellion.

You no longer need:

- Constant validation
- Excessive explanation
- Relentless productivity
- Overcompensation

Because your **energy speaks** louder than your résumé.

Your **aura walks in** before your name is called.

And that, dear one, is the true **power of alignment**.

Final Words: Let Radiance Lead

You were never meant to hide behind armor.

You were never meant to dim so others feel more comfortable.

You were never meant to fit in with frequencies that drain you.

You were meant to **light up rooms**, not with noise, but with truth.

So protect your energy, fiercely and lovingly.

Cleanse your soul, gently and consistently.

Expand your presence, not by effort, but by authenticity.

"You don't need to chase anymore.

You simply **arrive**, and everything begins to respond."

Because when your aura is aligned…

The universe recognizes you.

And the world,

finally

quietly

unmistakably

bows back.

9

Intuition, Synchronicity & Inner Guidance

The Lost Language of the Soul: What Is Intuition?

Intuition is not a gift, it's our original state before the noise took over.

There was a time, long before deadlines, notifications, and societal expectations, when you knew things without knowing how.

You could feel the truth of a situation.

You could sense when someone wasn't safe, even if they were smiling.

You were connected, not to facts, but to something far deeper: the silent wisdom of your soul.

That's intuition.

It's not magic. It's not superstition. It's your **original intelligence**, the GPS of your spirit.

It lives beneath the noise, beyond the mind, just waiting for you to remember it.

The Inner Compass vs. Overthinking

Intuition speaks instantly. Clearly.

It shows up as a whisper, a body sensation, or a sudden "I just know."

Overthinking comes later, with fear, logic, and doubt.

Intuition doesn't need to argue or explain.

It simply nudges.

If you miss it, it stays quiet. But if you listen… it can change your life.

Carl Jung called it the *collective unconscious*, the vast well of wisdom we all tap into when our ego steps aside.

In somatic healing, it's called the *felt sense*, your body's way of communicating truth before words can form.

And in mysticism, intuition is the **bridge between soul and self.**

> *"Intuition is perception beyond the five senses."* – Gary Zukav

That's why you can "feel" someone's energy the moment they enter a room.

Why you just *know* when to make a call, or when to walk away, or when something is about to shift, before anything physical has occurred.

How We Unlearn Our Inner Knowing

As children, we *know* who we like. We know when we're sad. We know what feels off.

But as we grow, we're taught to ignore these signals:

- **"Don't be dramatic."**
- **"Stop being sensitive."**
- **"Be practical."**

We're trained to seek answers externally, from experts, rules, systems.

And in that training, we forget how to trust ourselves.

But forgetting isn't the end. It's just the beginning of remembering.

Everyday Intuition Moments

You've felt it:

- You think of a friend and they text you minutes later.
- You feel a sudden urge to take a different route, and avoid an accident.

- You say yes to an opportunity even though it makes no sense, and it leads to your dream life.

- You walk away from someone "perfect on paper" because your gut whispered: *"No."*

That's not coincidence. That's inner guidance. And it's always available, if you pause and tune in.

Soul Practice: The 5-Second Gut Check

Before reacting, responding, or deciding, pause.

Close your eyes. Drop your attention from your mind to your body. Ask:

> **Does this feel expansive or contractive?**
>
> **Light or heavy? Open or tight?**

You'll know.

Even if the mind isn't ready, the soul always is.

Closing Insight

Intuition is not a gift for the lucky few.

It's the **native language of your soul.**

Before fear. Before logic. Before noise.

And every time you honor it, even in small ways, you reclaim your power.

You remember who you are.

> *"Your intuition will always whisper before life has to scream. Trust the whisper."*

2. Vibrations Don't Lie: Your Body as an Oracle

Theme: Intuition speaks through the body before it reaches the mind.

Your body is not just a vessel.

It's a **compass**, a **lie detector**, an **oracle**.

Before your mind begins to spin a story…

Before your ego builds logic or defense…

Your body already knows.

A tightening in your chest.

A sudden headache around a certain person.

Butterflies when you're about to say yes to something that lights you up.

Or that deep, dull ache when something's just not right, even if you can't explain why.

These are not random signals.

They are sacred communications.

Gabor Maté and the Wisdom of Trauma

Dr. Gabor Maté, a pioneer in trauma research, teaches that *"the body always says no, even when the mind says yes."*

When we suppress emotions, betray our needs, or overextend ourselves for others, the body stores the cost, through illness, inflammation, and chronic tension.

We may develop autoimmune diseases from years of unspoken grief.

We might suffer burnout not just from workload, but from soul-alignment fatigue.

Why?

Because the body *keeps score*, even when the mind forgets.

Stories We've All Lived

You've likely felt it too:

- Saying yes to a project, and instantly feeling exhausted or heavy in your chest.

- Ignoring a weird gut sensation about someone, only to be betrayed later.

- Feeling tension before an accident, or peace before a huge life shift.

- Meeting someone new and feeling your nervous system relax, without a word spoken.

And perhaps, moments when you *listened*,

You walked away, you waited, you paused, and everything changed for the better.

That wasn't luck. That was your body acting as your soul's messenger.

The "Felt Sense" and Inner Knowing

Eugene Gendlin, philosopher and psychologist, called this the **"felt sense."**

It's not just emotion. It's not thought.

It's that deep, pre-verbal awareness that something inside you *knows*.

In his Focusing method, you're taught to gently ask your body:

> "How does this situation feel… inside?"

> Not analyze it. Not judge it. Just *feel it*.

It's like a sacred pause, allowing your intuition to speak before the noise of logic enters.

When the Energy Is Off

In spiritual energy work, physical symptoms often carry energetic meaning:

- **Nausea** = rejection of something your soul doesn't want.

- **Tight neck and shoulders** = feeling burdened or repressed.

- **Sudden fatigue** = energetic intrusion or resistance.

- **Headaches** = conflict between logic and truth.

- **Stomach tightness** = lack of safety or hidden fear.

The body *never lies.*

It speaks in vibrations long before the truth becomes obvious.

Soul Practice: The 3-Point Body Scan

Whenever you're unsure about something, a person, decision, or opportunity, try this:

1. Heart:

Does your chest feel open or tight? Peaceful or restless?

2. Gut:

Is there a clench, a flutter, a nausea, or a calmness?

3. Breath:

Are you breathing freely, or is your breath shallow and constricted?

Then ask:

> "What is my body trying to tell me that my mind has not yet understood?"

Sit with the answer. It will come, not in words, but in *knowing*.

Closing Insight

The body is the interface between the seen and the unseen.

It senses truth faster than logic.

It carries messages from your intuition, your ancestors, your divine self.

So don't numb it. Don't rush it.

Listen.

Because sometimes, your soul speaks not in visions, but in chills, heartbeats, tension, and release.

> *"Your body whispers before it screams. Listen to the whisper."*

3. Synchronicity: When the Universe Speaks in Symbols

There are no accidents, only alignment or disconnection.

Sometimes the universe doesn't speak in words.

It speaks in symbols.

In birds that arrive at the exact moment you're questioning everything.

In repeating numbers that show up on clocks, license plates, receipts.

In overheard conversations, lyrics on the radio, or a child's smile when you most needed it.

This isn't coincidence.

It's **synchronicity**, the language of alignment.

Carl Jung's Definition

Swiss psychologist **Carl Jung** coined the term *synchronicity* to describe "meaningful coincidences", events that are not causally related but connected by meaning.

He believed we are all connected to a **collective unconscious**, a spiritual matrix, and when we are in harmony with it, life responds.

Jung wrote:

> "Synchronicity is an ever-present reality for those who have eyes to see."

It's not magic. It's resonance.

When your inner frequency matches your outer world, signs begin to emerge.

My Story: The Child's Smile

There was a time when everything in my life felt numb, emotionally, spiritually, even physically.

No clarity, no energy, no forward movement.

In desperation, I looked up and said:

> "God, if you're still with me… just show me a sign.
> I don't need a miracle. Just something small."

Later that day, I was walking on the street when a little child, a complete stranger, looked straight at me and smiled.

But not just any smile.

It felt like this child *saw* me. Through all the noise. Through all the heaviness.

And something in me melted.

It was subtle. But undeniable.

That moment was a *response*.

A confirmation that the universe was still listening.

And it changed me.

Reader Reflections (or Reader Inserts)

You've felt this too:

- You think of a friend, and they call.
- You see 11:11 or 222 every time you're about to make a big decision.

- You're grieving, and suddenly a white feather floats into view.

- You're confused about your purpose, and a billboard flashes a line that hits straight in the heart.

- You ask for a sign, and a butterfly lands on your hand. Or a stranger says the exact words you needed.

These are not just random. They are **echoes** from something higher, your higher self, Source, God, the field of consciousness, guiding you back home.

As *Laura Lynne Jackson* writes in *Signs*:

> "The universe is always speaking to us. All we need to do is open our hearts and listen."

Paulo Coelho and the Language of the World

In *The Alchemist*, Paulo Coelho writes:

> "When you want something, all the universe conspires in helping you to achieve it."

The protagonist learns to trust omens, patterns, feelings, "coincidences", as signs from the Soul of the World.

The message: **Your life is not random. It's a conversation.**

The more conscious you become, the more fluent you become in its language.

How to Recognize Synchronicity

- It feels **meaningful**, even if you can't explain why.

- It often comes in threes or repetition.

- It matches what you were just thinking, praying, or wondering.

- It brings **peace**, **goosebumps**, or a quiet certainty.

And most importantly, it often arrives when you *let go*.

Soul Practice: Sign Journal

Take a moment. Reflect on the last few days.

Write down three moments that felt "too timed" to be random.

Then ask:

- **What was I feeling before this sign appeared?**

- **What might this be pointing me toward?**

- **Am I willing to trust it, even if I don't fully understand it yet?**

Make this a habit.

The more you pay attention, the more signs will come.

Because the universe speaks more when it knows you're listening.

Closing Thought

You don't have to decode everything.

You don't have to force meaning into every moment.

Just trust the rhythm.

Because synchronicity isn't about control, it's about surrender.

> *"The universe leaves breadcrumbs for those who walk with faith."*

4. Inner Dialogue: Building Trust With Your Higher Self

Theme: The voice of intuition is quiet because it's sacred. It doesn't beg for attention, it waits for your trust.

We often expect divine guidance to be loud, dramatic, unmistakable.

But the voice of your Higher Self doesn't shout.

It **whispers**, gently, consistently, like a compass buried under the noise.

Not because it's weak… but because it's **sacred**.

It doesn't demand your obedience.

It waits for your trust.

Who Is the Higher Self?

Your Higher Self is not outside you. It *is* you, the timeless, wise, expanded part of you that sees beyond fear, survival, and ego stories.

It guides you not with commands, but with **nudges**, **dreams**, **longings**, and sometimes… resistance.

> As Gary Zukav puts it in *The Seat of the Soul*:
>
> "The alignment of your personality with your soul is authentic power."

When you follow your Higher Self, you're not chasing approval, you're choosing alignment.

It leads you to the life you came here to live, not the one others expect you to perform.

The Way It Speaks

You've heard it before.

- That quiet gut pull that said, "Don't go."
- That whisper during a heartbreak: "You'll grow from this."
- That knowing before an idea even forms: "This is for you."

Sometimes it's through dreams.

Sometimes through friction, when everything you *think* you want starts falling apart.

Divine resistance is often protection. The delay you're angry at may be grace in disguise.

But here's the truth:

Most of us don't follow it, not because we don't hear it, but because we **doubt it**.

Fear vs. Soul-Knowing

Fear is loud. It shouts worst-case scenarios.

The Higher Self is quiet, but firm. It holds steady, even when fear screams.

How to tell them apart?

Fear	Soul-Knowing
Contracts your chest	Expands your heart
Urges you to act now out of panic	Invites patience and timing
Seeks approval	Seeks truth
Feels like noise	Feels like peace under the noise

As *Michael A. Singer* writes in *The Untethered Soul*:

> "There is nothing more important to true growth than realizing you are not the voice of the mind."

You are the **awareness** listening beneath the noise.

Why We Ignore the Inner Voice

Because we've been conditioned to:

- Seek advice before seeking silence
- Choose logic over feeling
- Please others before pleasing ourselves
- Fear mistakes more than missing alignment

But every time you override your inner voice, you disconnect a little more from yourself.

And every time you trust it, even once, your inner world becomes louder than the outer.

Soul Practice: Mirror Conversation

Tonight, stand in front of a mirror. Look into your own eyes, not to judge, but to *listen*.

Say out loud:

> "What do I already know... but haven't trusted yet?"

Then wait.

Don't try to force an answer. Feel it rise.

You might hear words.

You might feel a sensation, a tightness, a relief, a tear.

You might just know.

Whatever shows up, trust it.

Write it down.

Act on it if you feel ready.

Repeat this often. It will rewire the bridge between you and your soul.

Closing Thought

You are not disconnected, just distracted.

And when you quiet the noise, you'll realize…

The voice you've been searching for has been with you all along.

It's not dramatic. It's not desperate.

It's simply **truth**, waiting for you to come home.

> *"The Higher Self doesn't need to be proven. It just needs to be trusted."*

5. Silence, Symbols & Sacred Listening

Theme: Intuition strengthens in stillness and sacred attention.

There is a reason spiritual masters, monks, shamans, and mystics across traditions value **silence**.

Not just as absence of noise, but as **presence of depth**.

In a world where we're addicted to stimulation, silence becomes radical.

It becomes the gateway through which the subtle speaks.

Why Silence Is a Spiritual Technology

Silence is not emptiness. It's a space where **energy becomes audible**.

> In *The Surrender Experiment*, Michael A. Singer wrote:
>
> *"The natural flow of life is the highest intelligence."*
>
> But to hear it, you must stop interfering, stop filling every gap with your agenda.

Silence allows your **inner ear** to open, where insight, guidance, and symbols rise.

It's where:

- The body reveals truth before the mind analyzes.
- Dreams download messages that waking logic blocks.

- Patterns become visible, repeating words, numbers, phrases you kept brushing off.

The Language of the Subtle Realms

The universe doesn't always speak in sentences. It whispers in:

- **Dreams** that replay a message you're ignoring

- **Birds, butterflies, feathers** that show up just when you're contemplating something important

- **Animals** crossing your path, a black dog during grief, a snake before transformation

- **Songs** that answer your questions

- **Cloud shapes**, **moon cycles**, or even **lost objects reappearing** mysteriously

You may call it coincidence. But when you start listening… you'll feel it's not.

> Indigenous wisdom teaches: *Nature is not scenery. It's scripture.*

Sacred Listening Isn't Passive, It's Attentive

This kind of listening isn't waiting for angels to appear.

It's **being fully present** to everything that already is.

Try this:

- Sit with a tree and ask it a question. Wait.
- Wake from a dream and write the first sentence that comes to mind.
- Hear the same phrase three times in a week? Look deeper.

Everything becomes a mirror. Every interaction becomes a message.

This is how shamans, tribal elders, or even children receive intuitive insight, not by force, but by attunement.

Don't Force Signs. Surrender to Them.

There's a difference between **seeking** signs and being **open** to them.

The ego begs for reassurance.

The soul trusts that guidance will come when needed.

> "Surrender is the highest form of listening," wrote Singer.
>
> When you stop forcing outcomes, you begin to move in harmony with what's already unfolding.

Let life surprise you. Let it meet you halfway.

Practice: 24-Hour Sacred Silence Challenge

- Turn off your phone (or keep it on Do Not Disturb)
- No social media, no news, no unnecessary talking
- Spend time in nature, journaling, or just being with yourself

Carry a small notebook. Whenever you notice a sign, feeling, or message, write it down.

At the end of the day, reflect: What came through when the world went quiet?

Closing Reflection

The divine doesn't compete for your attention, it waits for your attention.

Every sign, every whisper, every synchronicity is a reminder:

You are already connected to something greater. You've just forgotten how to listen.

> *"Stillness is the altar of spirit." – Paramahansa Yogananda*

6. Intuition in Decision-Making: Soul Over Strategy

Not every *smart* decision is *wise*. Some paths don't make sense until you walk them.

We're taught to calculate, compare, plan, and predict.

But the most meaningful decisions in life, the ones that shift your entire reality, often don't make *sense* at first. They make **soul**.

We know this truth deep down:

You can make the *right* decision on paper and still feel wrong inside.

You can follow every rule and still feel empty.

Because logic analyzes.

But **intuition aligns.**

> "Logic will get you from A to B. Imagination will take you everywhere." – Albert Einstein

And intuition, your soul's whisper, is the voice of that deeper intelligence.

When Strategy Fails, Soul Must Lead

Let's be clear: **strategy isn't the enemy.** It's necessary.

But strategy without soul leads to:

- Burnout in careers that once looked perfect
- Relationships that are safe but not sacred
- Success that feels hollow

Real wisdom is integrating both:

- **Logic plans the journey**

- Intuition chooses the direction

A Soul-Led Decision Feels Different

When you're tuned in, your body, emotions, and energy field will give you clues.

Here's how to begin discerning what your intuition is really saying:

Ask yourself:

1. **Does this drain or energize me?**

2. Not "Is this easy?" but "Does this feel alive?"

3. Expansion = Soul. Contraction = Ego or fear.

4. **Would I still do this if no one clapped?**

5. This filters out external validation.

6. If you'd do it in silence, it might be your truth.

7. **Is this fear pretending to be logic?**

8. Fear often dresses up as "practicality."

9. Ask: Am I moving toward love or away from discomfort?

Failures From Ignoring Intuition

- That job offer you took just because it paid well… and you ended up miserable.

- That relationship you stayed in because it looked good on the outside… but your gut screamed "no."

- That project you didn't start because you were afraid, and someone else did it instead, successfully.

We've all been there. And it's okay. Because every time you ignore your intuition, you *sharpen* your ability to recognize it the next time.

Wins From Following It Anyway

- The move to a new city that didn't make sense… but transformed your life.

- Saying yes to a creative project that "wasn't logical"… but led to massive growth.

- Walking away from "security"… and finding purpose on the other side.

You'll never regret honoring your truth, even if it's hard at first.

> "Sometimes what makes no sense at all is the only thing that truly makes you come alive."

Exercise: The Alignment Grid

Draw two columns in your journal.

Column A: "What I *could* do (logic)"

Column B: "What I *feel called* to do (intuition)"

Example:

Logic Says	Intuition Says
Stay in this stable job	Start that course you secretly love
Say yes to this collaboration	Say no, it feels off
Wait for a "better" time	Begin now, even if it's messy

Look at both.

Now ask: "Which of these paths would I regret *not* taking?"

You'll know.

Final Thought

You can calculate a thousand scenarios…

But the soul speaks in only one language: **truth.**

And truth isn't always loud.

Sometimes, it's just a whisper that says:

> "Go. You're ready. Even if you don't feel like it."

And you are.

7. Divine Timing, Surrender & the Signs You're Guided

When logic collapses, guidance takes over. All you have to do is listen and allow.

There are moments when no amount of planning, pushing, or perfecting works. When every door you try to force open remains shut. In those moments, you're not being punished. You're being paused.

The ego calls it delay.

The soul knows it as **divine timing.**

We've been trained to value control, to move fast, to decide quickly, to always know what's next. But true guidance isn't loud. It isn't on a clock. And it rarely reveals the full map.

Real guidance reveals only the **next step.** That's it. You don't need to see the whole staircase. Just take the one step that appears, and trust what comes next will rise to meet you.

There's a mantra worth remembering:

"Not control, but clarity. Not speed, but synchronicity."

Control is the mind's obsession.

Clarity is the soul's invitation.

Speed is often ego dressed as urgency.

But synchronicity flows in rhythm with divine will.

In sacred texts and real life, divine timing is a constant presence.

In the *Ramayana*, Rama's exile seemed like a tragedy. But it wasn't punishment, it was preparation. His time in the forest wasn't a detour. It was his spiritual path unfolding, aligning him with dharma, and preparing him for greater leadership.

In the life of Jesus, the crucifixion looked like defeat. But it was the exact point of resurrection. Suffering wasn't the end, it was the gateway to transcendence. What looked like collapse was, in truth, divine alignment in motion.

In our own lives, the same pattern plays out. A breakup that shattered you was also your freedom. A job loss that wrecked your plans cleared space for your calling. The illness, the failure, the delay, all of it, in hindsight, carried a deeper design.

When things fall apart, it's often grace, not punishment.

There was a time when life felt heavy and hopeless. I had reached a point where no effort seemed to work. Everything was stuck. I felt invisible. Emotionally drained. Spiritually dry.

One day, in quiet desperation, I whispered, "God… if you're still with me, show me. Just a sign."

Later that day, I passed a child on the street. A stranger, maybe three years old. The child looked straight at me and smiled. Not just a polite smile, it was a knowing, soft, radiant smile. The kind of smile that sees you. That understands without words. And in that moment, something inside me softened. It wasn't dramatic, but it was sacred.

That child's smile was the sign I asked for, not in lightning or thunder, but in silence and stillness. It was grace in human form. It reminded me that even when I feel forgotten, I am being held.

You are being guided, always. But guidance doesn't shout. It doesn't panic. It waits for your presence, your openness, your willingness to surrender.

Surrender is not giving up.

Surrender is saying: "I trust there's a deeper rhythm, even if I don't see it right now."

The path of surrender leads you to grace.

Closing Affirmation for Chapter 9:

> "I am guided by something deeper than reason, a knowing older than time. I don't need all the answers. I only need the courage to listen, follow, and trust that what I seek is also seeking me."

10

Service, Giving Back & Community

1. From Wound to Offering: Why You Were Chosen to Serve

There comes a moment in every healing journey when the pain that once felt like a curse begins to shimmer with a quiet purpose. What once broke you now teaches you. What once silenced you now gives you language. This is the sacred transmutation, where suffering doesn't vanish, but transforms. Where the wound becomes the doorway. The ache becomes the invitation. And the story you once wanted to hide becomes someone else's lifeline.

Michael Meade writes that within every wound lies a hidden gift. This gift isn't obvious. It's not wrapped in glory. It comes slowly, after the tears and the breakdowns, when you finally realize: you didn't survive for nothing. You went through what you went through so you could carry medicine no one else can. Not by fixing people. Not by preaching. But by being fully, vulnerably, honestly yourself.

The world doesn't need more saviors. It needs witnesses. People who are willing to show up with their truth intact, not in spite of what they've endured, but because of it. Your service doesn't have to be loud. It doesn't have to be public. Your very presence, when anchored in truth, becomes healing. The way you listen. The way you validate someone else's silent storm. The way you say, "Me too. I've been there."

Your scars are not shameful. They're proof you survived. And someone needs to see that survival is possible.

Healing isn't the end of the story. It's the beginning of service. It's the moment you stop asking, "Why did this happen to me?" and start asking, "How can this help someone else feel less alone?" That's when the wound becomes wisdom. That's when your story becomes a gift.

Now, ask yourself: What have I survived that shaped me? And how might it now be someone else's survival guide? Not to impress. Not to rescue. But to remind another soul: healing is possible, and they are not alone. In this way, your presence becomes a prayer, one only you could embody.

2. Soul-Service vs. Ego-Help: The Spiritual Integrity of Giving

Real service uplifts both giver and receiver, without control, pity, or superiority.

True service is not about fixing others. It's about being present with them in their humanity, their struggle, their sacred unfolding, without trying to control the outcome. This is the difference between ego-help and soul-service. One inflates the self. The other dissolves it.

In ego-help, giving becomes a subtle performance. It seeks applause, recognition, or the feeling of superiority that comes from being needed. It wears the mask of kindness but is often rooted in unhealed patterns, the desire to be validated, to be indispensable, to be seen as "good." At its core, ego-help doesn't serve the other person's highest good. It serves the helper's emotional agenda. It says, "Let me save you," often without asking if saving is what the other truly needs.

Soul-service, by contrast, is quiet. Grounded. It arises from overflow, from a heart that has seen its own darkness and is no longer afraid of others'. It doesn't try to rescue, because it honors the sovereignty of the other soul. It doesn't offer unsolicited advice or energy. It listens. It holds. It reflects. As Mark Nepo writes, "Help is not fixing. It is holding." Soul-service is less about doing and more about being, being a safe, honest, compassionate presence that reminds others of their own light, not of your own.

In this way, soul-service is deeply spiritual. It demands inner clarity. Before extending your hand, it asks you to pause and ask yourself: *Am I giving from fullness or from a wound? Am I offering from genuine care or from a need to be needed?*

Energetic consent is another pillar of true service. Not everyone wants to be helped. Not everyone is ready to be seen. And trying to force transformation before its time can be a form of spiritual aggression. Soul-service respects timing, autonomy, and choice. It trusts that each soul has its own divine curriculum, and that your role is not to alter it, but to support it, if and only if you're invited.

When we give from ego, there is often an unspoken hierarchy, "I have what you lack." This creates imbalance, shame, dependency. But when we give from soul, there is equality. The roles dissolve. The giver and the receiver both expand. The exchange becomes sacred. Both are changed.

True service is reciprocal in energy. You may not receive something tangible in return, but you'll always feel uplifted, because you gave without attachment, and without agenda. There's a quiet joy in that. A purity. A peace.

The world is full of helpers. But what we need are vessels, people who serve not to be seen, but to see. Who serve not to save, but to love.

So, before you give, pause and ask: "Is this love or performance? Is this overflow or obligation? Am I showing up to control... or to witness?"

Because when giving is aligned with your soul, it doesn't deplete, it radiates.

3. The Power of Small Circles: Community as Spiritual Practice.

You don't need a stage, a mic, or a million followers to make a difference. Sometimes, the most powerful transformations happen in the quiet of small rooms, in whispered truths, over chai with a friend, or through a late-night message that simply says, "I'm here."

This is the power of small circles, not just as connection, but as a spiritual practice.

Real community isn't loud. It doesn't parade itself on social media. It often lives in subtle gestures:

– A friend who checks in without a reason.

– Someone who holds space while you cry without rushing to fix you.

– The courage to speak your messy, raw truth in front of someone you trust, and not feel judged for it.

These moments may seem small, but they hold **soul-level power**. They remind us that we are not alone, that we matter, and that healing isn't a solitary path, it's a shared one.

Bell Hooks once wrote, *"Love is an action, never simply a feeling."*

In a world that prizes self-sufficiency and performative perfection, showing up for others with presence, honesty, and consistency is revolutionary. Community becomes an act of love, not romantic love, but the spiritual kind that builds bridges and breaks isolation.

In spiritual growth, we often think of retreats, gurus, or big groups. But most breakthroughs don't happen in crowds. They happen in **safe, small spaces** where we can drop the mask.

Where we can say:

"I'm not okay today."

"I'm scared, but I still showed up."

"I celebrated something and wanted someone to know."

And when someone replies, "Me too. I see you.", something profound happens. Shame softens. Courage grows. You rise.

This is why mutual support, not hierarchy, is the new spirituality. We don't need more gurus on pedestals. We need humans willing to be honest, present, and real with each other.

You don't need to be anyone's healer. You just need to be available for truth.

Start your own Soul Circle, and don't overthink it. It's simpler than you think:

1. **Find one or two people** you trust and feel emotionally safe with.

2. **Pick one day a week** to connect, in person, on call, or over voice notes.

3. **Create a sacred space**: This is not a gossip session. It's a truth-sharing container.

4. **Each person gets 5–10 minutes** to share what they're feeling, moving through, or celebrating. No advice unless asked. Just listening.

5. **Close with a single sentence:** "Today, I felt seen when…" or "What I'm taking with me is…"

That's it.

No fancy rituals. No pressure to fix. Just sacred presence.

The magic isn't in the structure, it's in the sincerity.

So don't wait for the perfect group. Start with one person.

Build slow. Let truth lead. And over time, that little circle will become a sacred fire, warm enough to melt fear, and bright enough to guide each other home.

4. Manifestation Through Alignment: Becoming the Frequency

True manifestation isn't about visualizing harder, repeating affirmations 55 times, or writing your desires in glitter pens under a full moon.

It's about frequency.

About becoming a living, breathing match for what you say you want.

That's the core teaching behind masters like *Abraham Hicks*, *Joe Dispenza*, and *Neville Goddard*.

They each speak, in their own language, about one truth: **you don't manifest what you want, you manifest what you are.**

And what you are is a vibration.

So let's dismantle the shallow version of manifestation, the one obsessed with quick fixes, vision boards, and scripting without embodiment.

It may feel good temporarily, but if your nervous system is still stuck in lack, if your thoughts are rooted in "not enough," if your body carries unprocessed fear… you'll repel the very thing you're trying to attract.

You can't fake frequency.

If you want peace, but your day is filled with anxiety, urgency, and control, you're not aligned.

If you want love, but you abandon your own needs constantly, you're not ready to receive what you're craving.

If you want freedom, but you keep saying yes out of fear, you're still in energetic bondage.

Joe Dispenza says, *"You have to become the energy of your future."*

Neville Goddard reminds us, *"Assume the feeling of the wish fulfilled."*

Abraham Hicks adds, *"Everything you want is downstream. Stop paddling upstream."*

This means: stop striving. Start **tuning**.

And this is where your **nervous system** comes in.

Many of us are carrying trauma that wires us for survival, not expansion.

Your body might not feel safe to hold wealth, love, visibility, or joy.

So even when the opportunities come, you unconsciously sabotage, delay, or downplay them, because a part of you doesn't believe it's safe, sustainable, or real.

So the work isn't just to visualize the future.

It's to **regulate yourself into readiness.**

Ask daily:

"What emotion does my future hold?"

If your dream life holds freedom, excitement, ease, or impact, ask:

"How can I feel just a little bit of that today?"

Not in fantasy.

In embodiment.

Can you take one small action that signals safety and alignment?

Can you pause for five minutes and breathe into joy, not because something amazing happened, but because you chose to hold that frequency anyway?

Manifestation isn't magic.

It's alignment.

It's becoming the kind of person who naturally lives in the reality you're calling in.

When you live as if it's already yours, not pretending, but embodying, the universe doesn't have to be convinced.

It simply **matches** you.

So don't just ask for the thing.

Become the version of you who can hold it.

That's when manifestation stops being a "technique"…

And starts becoming your **natural state.**

5. Co-Creation: The Universe Responds to Who You've Become

Manifestation begins with desire, but it doesn't end there.

Desire is the spark. But becoming… that's the fire.

You don't manifest by setting a goal and hoping the universe fills in the blanks.

You **co-create** by stepping into alignment with the identity that goal requires.

Every dream demands a version of you.

Not the idealized, perfect version.

But the consistent, courageous one, who makes small, meaningful shifts every day.

This is the path:

Intention → Identity → Integrity → Inspired Action.

1. Intention:

You start by asking clearly: *What do I want?*

Be honest. Not what sounds good, what your soul actually longs for.

2. Identity:

Next, ask: *Who do I need to become in order to live that reality?*

If your dream is to be a calm, successful, heart-led creator, then your identity isn't "someone trying to survive."

It's "someone who chooses peace. Someone who honors their vision even on small days."

As James Clear writes in *Atomic Habits*:

"Every action you take is a vote for the type of person you wish to become."

So identity isn't fixed. It's shaped, one vote at a time.

3. Integrity:

You stay aligned by making your daily choices match your inner vision.

This is about self-trust, not perfection.

Can your thoughts, words, and actions line up, even when no one's watching?

Because integrity creates spiritual gravity.

When your energy is clean, life starts flowing toward you with less resistance.

4. Inspired Action:

This is the surrender + movement dance.

As Michael A. Singer writes in *The Surrender Experiment*, life is always guiding us, not through force, but through subtle invitations.

Your job isn't to control everything.

It's to show up for what life places in front of you, with full presence, and take the next best step.

Because **the universe doesn't respond to what you want. It responds to who you've become.**

And it responds through synchronicities, openings, relationships, ideas, and timing, often when you least expect it.

In my own life, every major turning point, the job that felt right, the friend who changed everything, the opportunity that seemed tailor-made, didn't arrive when I was chasing.

They arrived when I shifted internally.

When I started **living like it was already mine.**

Not faking. Not pretending.

But carrying the energy, habits, and posture of someone who believed in their own becoming.

That's co-creation.

You take one aligned step.

The universe echoes back with ten more.

Practice:

Write a letter from your Future Self.

Not a fantasy version, but a grounded, embodied one.

Write from the voice of the You who is already living the life you now desire.

Include:

- What daily habits helped you evolve?
- What mindset did you let go of?
- How did you respond when things got hard?
- What kind of energy do you carry now?

- What truths do you wish your past self had trusted earlier?

This letter becomes a map, not to control your future, but to meet it with clarity.

Because once you start becoming...

The path becomes inevitable.

6. Dharma & Devotion: Living As a Channel, Not a Chaser

Dharma is not about becoming something great, it's about *remembering who you already are at the soul level*, and aligning your life with that truth.

In the Vedic tradition, **dharma** means "righteous path" or "right action", not as dictated by society or ambition, but by the subtle intelligence of your soul's blueprint. It is the essence of what you are here to *do*, not just for yourself, but as your offering to the world.

Dharma is not the same as passion.

Passion is often driven by emotion and excitement, it can fluctuate with mood, trends, or energy.

Dharma is deeper. It's the work that keeps calling you, even when it's inconvenient, even when no one claps, even when it's hard.

Purpose is how we often name what feels meaningful.

Dharma is the sacred commitment to *live* that meaning out, through action, consistency, and service.

Think of it like this:

- **Passion** says: "I want to feel good doing this."
- **Purpose** says: "This matters to me deeply."
- **Dharma** says: "I will do it, because it is mine to do, and the doing itself is holy."

The **Bhagavad Gita** beautifully illustrates this through the dialogue between Krishna and Arjuna.

Arjuna is paralyzed by doubt, unsure if he should fight the battle ahead.

Krishna reminds him: *"Better to fail in your own dharma than to succeed in another's."*

He teaches: *Act, but without attachment to outcomes.* Let your duty be your offering, not your ego's achievement.

This is where **devotion** enters.

Dharma becomes alive when we offer our work not for applause, but as a sacred act of service.

You don't need to be a monk, healer, or artist to live in dharma.

You can sweep a floor, design a building, raise a child, write a letter, or build a business, all as dharma, *if it's aligned and offered in devotion.*

Living in dharma doesn't mean you never struggle.

But it means even your struggle feels meaningful, because you know you're walking the path meant for you.

Devotion gives your actions spiritual weight.

You move from chasing outcomes to *channeling* truth.

From proving yourself to *serving the moment*.

From performing to *praying through action*.

Your life becomes less about "How much can I get?" and more about "How deeply can I give what I came here to give?"

Practice

Each morning, before checking your phone or planning your tasks, close your eyes and say softly:

"Let my actions be in alignment, not ambition. Let me be of service today."

Then move through your day not to impress, but to *express* what's real, true, and yours to offer.

When you live this way, the right doors open. The right people find you. And your soul finally exhales, because it remembers why it came.

7. Embodiment: Becoming the Aligned You, Every Day

At the end of every journey, you're not meant to just look back and admire the view, you're meant to *become* the view. Not to just understand the path, but to *walk* it. To feel the teachings in your breath, your voice, your choices.

The final teaching is simple.

It's not about gaining more insight.

It's not about perfecting your practice.

It's about one thing: **embodiment.**

To embody means to take everything you've remembered, your intuition, presence, truth, compassion, awareness, and wear it as your *skin*. Not just in your mind or journal, but in your posture, your words, your daily rhythm.

You don't have to transcend anything.

You don't have to become someone else.

You just have to **be**, more fully, more honestly, more aligned with who you truly are.

The highest form of spirituality is not how still you sit in meditation…

It's how you treat the person in front of you.

It's how you respond when things fall apart.

It's how you breathe when no one is watching.

It's easy to feel awakened on a retreat, in silence, or while reading these pages.

The real work, and the real gift, is bringing that light into ordinary moments:

Waiting in line.

Washing dishes.

Saying no kindly.

Resting without guilt.

Creating from your heart, not your ego.

This is **spiritual embodiment**:

- Not what you *say* you believe, but how you *show up*.
- Not how deeply you understand the path, but how gently you walk it.
- Not how loudly you speak truth, but how quietly you *live* it.

You are not here to become perfect.

You are here to become real.

Because in the end, you are not the student or the seeker anymore,

You are the message.

You are the prayer.

You are the light.

And the world doesn't need more enlightened words,

It needs more *embodied souls*.

So what does that look like?

It looks like being gentle when you want to react.

It looks like choosing love when fear feels louder.

It looks like aligning with your higher self, even when no one's watching.

The path is not linear, it is circular.

You'll return again and again: to lessons, to emotions, to truths you thought you'd mastered.

But each time, you'll come back wiser, softer, more embodied.

And slowly, this won't be something you remember only in quiet moments,

It will be how you *live*.

Daily Ritual: The 10-Minute Alignment Practice

Make this your daily return to Self, your anchor in an ever-shifting world. You can do this morning or evening. Adjust as needed. But do it with presence.

1. Mirror Work (2 mins)

Stand in front of the mirror. Look into your eyes.

Say: *"I see you. I trust you. I am proud of how far you've come."*

Let this be a meeting with your soul, not your surface.

2. Grounding Breath & Body Check (2 mins)

Sit or stand still. Inhale deeply, slowly.

Scan your body from head to toe.

Ask: *"Where am I holding tension?"*

Exhale. Let it go.

Ask: *"How do I feel right now, and what do I need?"*

3. Journaling or Reflection (3 mins)

Write (or say aloud):

- One thing I'm grateful for
- One truth I'm remembering
- One aligned step I will take today

4. Silence & Listening (2 mins)

No music. No movement. Just listen.

Let your soul speak, even if you hear nothing, trust that the listening is enough.

5. Affirmation or Mantra (1 min)

End with one of your own, or:

"I walk in truth. I move in peace. I am already whole."

That's it.

Ten minutes.

But if done with sincerity, it can shift your entire day.

And if you forget, that's okay.

You are not here to get it all right.

You're here to *return*.

Return to your truth.

Return to your breath.

Return to your higher self, again and again, until it no longer feels like a return… but simply, home.

This isn't the conclusion. It's the *integration*.

Not an ending, but a gentle beginning.

Now go live this.

Breathe it.

Create with it.

Serve through it.

And when you feel lost, don't look outside.

You already know the way.

It's within you.

It's always been.

You are the path.

You are the practice.

You are the presence.

Key Takeaways That Helped Me In Difficult Times

- **Your pain is not punishment, it's a portal.**
  My hardest moments became the doorway to my spiritual awakening.

- **The voice inside you is wiser than the world around you.**
  Intuition saved me when logic failed.

- **Surrender isn't giving up. It's giving in to a higher plan.**
  Letting go of control gave me peace I never knew I needed.

- **You don't have to be perfect to be powerful.**
  Showing up as I am, raw, real, flawed, connected me to my purpose.

- **Your aura speaks before you do. Protect it. Feed it.**
  I learned to clean my energy the way we clean our homes.

- **You're not going crazy. You're waking up.**
  Spiritual awakening often looks like falling apart before rising.

- **The Ego wants comfort. The Higher Self wants truth.**
  Choosing truth hurt sometimes, but it set me free.

- **You're never alone, your Higher Self walks with you.**
  I stopped searching outside and started listening within.

- **Synchronicities are love notes from the Universe.**
  They were my guiding lights in the dark.
- **Your story can heal others.**

  That's why I wrote this book, for me, for you, for all of us awakening.

10 Laws To Unlock Your Inner God And Find Your True Calling

1. **Awakening: The Divine Nudge**
   Every spiritual journey begins with a whisper from within, a deep inner call that something greater is waiting to be lived.

2. **The Inner War: Ego vs. Higher Self**
   Recognize the ongoing battle between your ego's fears and your Higher Self's truth. Growth begins with awareness of this war.

3. **Dark Night of the Soul: Breakdown Before Breakthrough**
   Transformation often begins in darkness. Your most painful moments are sacred catalysts for awakening.

4. **Truth: The Sword That Sets You Free**
   Honesty with yourself and others is the foundation of alignment. Truth pierces illusions and realigns you with your path.

5. **Letting Go: Releasing the Old You**
   Shedding limiting beliefs, toxic patterns, and false identities is essential for spiritual rebirth.

6. **Surrender: Trusting the Higher Plan**
   Real power comes from surrender, not weakness, but divine trust in what is unfolding.

7. **God Mode: Living in Flow and Energy**
   When aligned with your Higher Self, you enter flow, life moves through you with purpose, power, and peace.

8. **Compassion: The Energy of Love**
   Embrace deep feeling and vulnerability. Compassion for self and others expands your aura and unlocks divine presence.

9. **Intuition, Synchronicity & Inner Guidance**
   Your Higher Self communicates through inner knowing and outer signs. Tune in and follow the golden breadcrumbs.

10. **Embodiment: Becoming the Aligned You, Every Day**
    Mastery isn't in knowing, but in *being*. Your daily actions, energy, and presence reflect the god within.

Shukrana

This book is not just written,

It is *blessed*.

A humble **Shukrana** to all the readers who walked this journey of awakening with me. May these words stir your soul, expand your aura, and guide you home to your Higher Self.

This work is not mine alone.
It is the divine grace and blessing of my **Guruji**.

May his light flow through these pages,
And may it touch you in the exact moment you need it most.

Blessings Always — Guruji

www.ingramcontent.com/pod-product-compliance
Lightning Source LLC
Chambersburg PA
CBHW020325170426
43200CB00006B/281